Praise for *The Split*

The Split is a collection of personal stories from real women and mothers who have experienced being children, wives, mothers, and divorcees. A brutal reality for many modern women is that while life today looks nothing like it did 100 or 200 years ago, many of us still feel the invisible push and pull of societal and cultural expectations around matrimony and motherhood. For women at any point in the process who might be questioning their own experience, choices, or future path, stories of experience like these are supportive and helpful.

Experts in the business of divorce—lawyers, mediators, social workers—may hear hundreds of these stories a year, but for the women and families making these decisions and walking through the process of change and rebuilding, there is a common refrain: they feel shocked, alone, isolated, unsupported, and frequently embarrassed and ashamed.

A book like *The Split*, with these short but personal narratives of real people's experiences, is a helpful bridge. Those who might not otherwise know anybody in their own lives to look to for support will find comfort and the start of their own personal courage in these pages.

— **AMY STONE**, AUTHOR OF *BLEND*, CREATOR OF STEPPARENT SCHOOL, AND HOST OF THE POPULAR PODCAST *THE ART OF IMPERFECT ADULTING*

The Split is about way more than divorce. It's about what we as humans experience when facing the end of a big dream. It's the agony and the ecstasy of the human condition: cycling through painful endings and equally powerful beginnings. It's about the Phoenix in each of us, rising from the ashes and becoming a greater, freer version of ourselves. I found parts of who I have been and who I am becoming in each woman's story. Chances are, so will you.

— **FRANCES TREJO-LAY**, AWARD WINNING AUTHOR, ENERGY HEALER AND WOMEN'S CIRCLE FACILITATOR

The Split offers a much needed perspective on the always shifting face of relationships. An ending is often the blessed beginning of a new, more empowered chapter. Wise and hopeful.

— **MIMI RICH**, MA, MARRIAGE & FAMILY THERAPIST (RETIRED) AND AWARD WINNING AUTHOR

The Split is a compelling collection of stories that delve into one of life's most universal experiences, the moment something breaks and what follows after. Spanning a range of voices, styles, and emotional landscapes, this anthology examines both relationship splits and the broader fractures that shape a life: the end of a marriage, the unraveling of relationships, the loss of identity, and the unexpected detours that force us to reinvent ourselves.

As an attorney that deals with divisions as a daily occurrence, I can say what makes this anthology shine is its emotional honesty. Each author approaches "the split" from a fresh angle that is sometimes with quiet introspection and vulnerability. The stories refuse easy answers and instead they leave space for contradictions. The collection shares heartbreak that coexists with relief, grief intertwined with growth, and endings that become unlikely beginnings. Just like life.

The collection is beautifully balanced. Some stories linger in the ache of separation, immersing the reader in moments where love falters or futures dissolve. Others shift toward resilience and reconstruction, highlighting the strength required to start again. The result is an anthology that mirrors real life that is sometimes messy, multifaceted, but ultimately most important hopeful.

The variety of stories is a strength, but all evocative snapshots of people caught at crossroads. Yet despite the diversity, the stories feel cohesive, unified by the central theme of how we navigate change and what we discover about ourselves in the aftermath.

Perfect for readers who have or are dealing with the ending of relationships in their owns lives. *The Split* invites reflection on the struggles we've lived through and the ones that have yet to come. It's an anthology that lingers long after the final page because of its testament to human resilience.

— **RENA MCDONALD**, ATTORNEY AND AWARD WINNING AUTHOR OF *BECAUSE I CARE*

As a newly divorced middle-aged woman, whose parents, siblings, and grandparents have all had multiple marriages and divorces, I wanted to read stories that resonated with my experiences, and was not disappointed. Not only did I find common ground, I was able to see parts of myself in all of the writing. What became apparent is that, despite a wide variety of backgrounds, timelines, religions, sexual identities, and ages, I saw glimmers of hope shining through. *Split* does not mean broken Let me yell that out loud, "SPLIT DOES NOT MEAN BROKEN!" I am thankful that so many women dared to let us see into their histories, painful as it may have been to relive them. It helped me immensely to know that Brandee Melcher was also a parentified child who managed to heal despite some deeply rooted patterns. Carol Britton emphasized the bond between siblings raised in traumatic homes, reminding me again why my relationship with my sister is ultimately my most valued. Sierra Melcher's observation that "it takes two people to break up well" made me smile, knowing that I managed to extract my freedom from my ex-husband with our friendship remaining intact after almost three decades. LaToya Burdiss wrote about something that happens in many marriages, like my own, the silent unraveling of loose threads, "one by one" until it is just over. I am grateful to every woman who was brave enough to share their story in *The Split*. I hope that everyone; married, divorced or single will take the time to read this. It will provide insight and understanding to those who have gone before, and those who will end up divorced. Knowing more and feeling a kinship with others makes the healing happen faster, leading to a healthy future. Thank you!

— **LESLIE BARBER**, AWARD WINNING AUTHOR OF *FEISTY* AND *DEATH DAY* AND A DIVORCED MOM OF TWO ADULT SONS

The Split

TALES OF FAMILY RENEWAL AND FEMALE RESILIENCE

BRANDEE MELCHER   DR. KATHERINE HUMPHREYS

CAROL BRITTON   LESLEY GOTH, PSYD

CAROLINA CIFUENTES   CHRISTEN E. BRYCE

DR. ERICA ANNE LOVE   ALLISON BANEGAS

SUMMER JEAN   LATOYA BURDISS   JEN KENNEDY

SIERRA MELCHER

Copyright © 2025 by Red Thread Publishing LLC

All rights reserved.

No part of this book may be reproduced in any form or by any electronic or mechanical means, including information storage and retrieval systems, without written permission from the author, except for the use of brief quotations in a book review.

Red Thread Publishing LLC. 2025

Write to **info@redthreadbooks.com** if you are interested in publishing with Red Thread Publishing. Learn more about publications or foreign rights acquisitions of our catalog of books: www.redthreadbooks.com

Ebook ISBN: 979-8-89294-043-6

Paperback ISBN: 979-8-89294-042-9

Hardcover ISBN: 979-8-89294-044-3

DISCLAIMER:

The information and advice contained in this book are based upon the research and the personal and professional experiences of the authors. Some names and characteristics have been changed, some events have been compressed, and some dialogue has been recreated. Chapters reflect the authors' present recollections of experiences over time. The opinions herein are of each individual contributor. All writings are the property of individual contributors.

The publisher and authors are not responsible for any adverse effects or consequences resulting from the use of any of the suggestions, preparations, or procedures discussed in this book.

Contents

Trigger Warning Disclaimer — ix
Introduction — xi

1. TO BE RESCUED — 1
   Brandee Melcher

2. SWEPT UNDER THE RUG — 11
   Carol Britton

3. FINDING MY TRUE SELF IN THE SPLITS — 21
   Lesley Goth, PsyD

4. THERE IS NO SUCH THING AS A NORMAL FAMILY — 31
   Carolina Cifuentes

5. THE RADICAL REFRAME — 41
   Sierra Melcher

6. DICHOTOMY OF DIVORCE AND SELF-EMPOWERMENT — 51
   Summer Jean

7. HOW FAR? — 63
   Dr. Katherine Humphreys

8. LISTENING FOR GRACE — 71
   Dr. Erica Anne Love

9. I DEFINE ME — 81
   Allison Banegas

10. FAITH IN THE FIRE — 91
    Jen Kennedy, MPA

11. I NEVER BELONGED TO ONE WORLD — 101
    LaToya Burdiss

12. LIVING A LIE — 107
    Christen E. Bryce, MS, RN

Epilogue — 117

Thank You	119
Acknowledgments	121
Red Thread Publishing	123
Other Books	125

Trigger Warning Disclaimer

This book contains personal stories that address sensitive and potentially distressing topics, including divorce, sexual violence, rape, and family abuse. Reader discretion is advised.

These stories are shared with honesty and courage, with the intention of offering understanding, connection, and hope to others who have experienced or witnessed similar pain. Please take care while reading and honor your emotional well-being; pause or seek support if you need to.

Introduction

Did you hear? They're getting divorced...
His dad isn't around...
She's keeping the kids from him...
We have a broken family...

We've all heard these phrases whispered in hushed tones, so others might not hear, a hint of shame, disappointment, or judgment hanging in the air as the conversation continues. Hell, once upon a time, we may have even been the ones saying these things with our own form of judgment as someone's life seemingly crumbled around them. I know I said these phrases or similar ones when I was younger, less experienced in life, and before my own personal split.

These phrases, specifically the *broken family* comment, are what led me to pitch this book idea over two years ago.

Maybe it was the circles I was in or a universal alignment, but I was hearing the term *"broken families"* almost every other day, through social media, personal conversations, my children, and podcasts. Some people were claiming that title for themselves, others were contesting the narrative, and others were simply repeating what they had heard. Every time I heard that phrase, the irritation grew to frustration and then to anger as I gripped my steering wheel and yelled at the podcast host, *"WE'RE NOT FUCKING BROKEN!! FUCK YOU!!"*

I'm not usually one to get angry to the point of yelling, so why was this sticking with me so hard? Personally, I was 2 years past separation, 1 year as an official divorcee, and feeling better than I had in a very long time. I began thinking of my childhood, how I felt more broken and confused while my parents were married than when they divorced. I remember feeling like a shell of a person during the later years of my marriage, and how alive I feel now, divorced. I thought of all the women I knew who were divorced or single, and thought how much better their lives and their children's lives had become since separating from their long-term partners. This is not to say they were not without struggle and hard moments, *that* these difficult times were easier single than if they had stayed partnered. Arguably, *something* was broken *prior* to the split; otherwise, would the split have happened?

Splitting was the answer, NOT the problem.

The best part about this book? It demonstrates how the transformation from the original discussion of divorce to the current one acknowledges the different splits these women have experienced. The following stories are from women who recount stories of terminating relationships while acknowledging the various splits they have experienced in their lives, and how it has shaped them into who they are today.

Most importantly? These are NOT broken women.

These are strong, bold, resilient, courageous, and audacious women who decided they wanted more for themselves and were not going to simply accept what the world was willing to give to them. They decided to forge a new path for themselves, their families, and those who wish to follow.

To choose yourself is a bold declaration. To invite others to do the same is a path to collective healing.

We invite you to join us in changing the narrative around divorce and the complexities of life. These experiences are not shameful events meant to be hidden and discussed in hushed tones. These stories highlight the strength in sharing our fears and desires. Too often, women bear the responsibilities associated with family changes, and often, they manage these responsibilities alone. They quiet their desires, fears and needs in order to focus on the greater good of those around them. It is this quieting that fuels the social stigmas and allows shame to persist regarding the difficult decision to pursue more. As you'll read in the following stories, when these women took radical responsibility, their lives and those around them ultimately improved.

A profound "Thank you" and deep appreciation to Sierra Melcher and the entire Red Thread team for having patience as the universe aligned to bring this book to publication two years after the idea originally came to me.

A deep gratitude to all the authors who came forward to share their stories with the world and offer a place of connection. This could not have happened without your strength and vulnerability.

Centuries of social programming and policies have taught us that "splitting" is the final chapter of a woman's life and the ultimate collapse of a family unit. Experience provides a very different truth. We are here to share these truths with you. To let you know that you're *not* alone, you're *not* broken, and that there is a wonderful future ahead of you.

Splitting is not the end; it is simply one ending of one chapter in one book. I came across a quote on Instagram (@rewildingforwomen) that said, *'Endings are love in a different outfit.'* I couldn't agree more. Until it is your time to move onto the next realm, we invite you to embrace new experiences, splits and try on new outfits!

— *Brandee Melcher, Award winning author of* The Break

CHAPTER 1

To Be Rescued

BRANDEE MELCHER

Cowboy Take Me Away by The Chicks was playing on the radio, and I was singing my preteen heart out before being interrupted by my mother.

She said something to the effect of *"You only like this song because you want to be rescued."* I stared at her, quickly denying what she said, even though it was true. I didn't like that she was right, because no preteen daughter wants her mother to be right about anything. I also didn't want to admit she was right because I didn't want to admit I wanted to be rescued from her, from my father, from this family, from this life. At 11 or 12 years old, I shouldn't want to be rescued. I shouldn't want to leave my family. I shouldn't want to be as far away from the people who are *supposed* to help me feel the safest. But I did... because I wasn't safe.

Every day was a constant juggle. Which was the safe parent that day? Would there be a minor inconvenience that would cause my father to lose his temper and shatter a plastic ketchup bottle like it was glass, leaving me and my brothers to look to our mother for protection and guidance? Which wouldn't come because those two would become embroiled in an hours-long fight that would rage through the house. Or, would something about me trigger my mother's own self-hatred, which she'd take out on me? Causing me to look at the clock and wonder when my father would be home because at least she wouldn't hit me in front of him...mostly. My parents knew I received the majority of their aggression, judged each other for it, but that still didn't stop either one of them from falling back on verbal, emotional, physical or mental abuse.

They fought over their treatment of me, of my brothers, of finances, of distrust, past indiscretions, their parents... almost anything from a daily existence.

So yes, I did want to be rescued. I wanted to go somewhere that wasn't confusing. I wanted to be with people I knew wouldn't harm me. I wanted to be safe. I just didn't exactly know safety was what I was chasing, because being 11 years old in the mid-90s, there wasn't a vocabulary for this. In fact, I was sometimes viewed as the neighborhood problem child from a "*good*" family. I was obviously the problem since I ran away from home (to my friend's house), always had at least one brother in tow when playing, and was just generally awkward. My siblings were too young to be "problem children," and no one really knew what was going on once our front door shut. Of course, I was the problem. Luckily for us all, my parents finally divorced, or at least separated, by the time I was 13.

Over the previous two years, cops had been called, court had been attended, remedial punishments doled out... and the cycle continued until everything finally came to an end. The details are fuzzy; however, the main outcome was that my parents *finally and* permanently separated, and my mom and I moved to San Antonio, TX, in the middle of my freshman year of high school. While my mom wasn't an entirely safe adult, she was safer than my father in a sense. I also knew that by living with her, I wouldn't have to take care of my younger brothers. I didn't realize I would be trading the care-taking of two children for becoming a parentified child to my mother. Parents are supposed to take care of their pre-teen children, not the other way around. Either way, I saw Texas as a new beginning, and all the problems from the past were not going to follow me.

∼

To say that Texas was a fresh start is misleading. It was fresh in that it was a new place, somewhere no one in our road trip caravan had been before. This caravan included: me, my mom, her significantly younger boyfriend, his brother, my mom's neighborhood friend, and her military boyfriend. The ages ranged from 14 years old (me) to my 31-year-old mom; everyone else was in their late teens to late twenties. While the youngest of the group, I sometimes felt like I was the oldest, both physically *and* mentally. I saw parts of the country I may never see again, and felt a bit of freedom. My mom was distracted by her new love, so I was left to my own devices. Not that there was much I could do besides think my mom's boyfriend's brother was cute. He was cute, older and thus a mild flirtation began between us on the road trip. The mild flirtation turned into kisses and some over-the-clothes touching. Nothing inappropriate for two 14-year-olds to be doing. Only, he was 18. And completely inappropriate.

My mom, in an attempt to be a mother, scolded me, attempted to ground me and ultimately left the situation alone since he would be leaving back to Maryland once we were settled in Texas. I believed that once we were settled things would get better.

I believed my mom and I would become friends, the fighting would end, I'd continue to excel in school, graduate with honors, and all of the troubles of Maryland would be left behind. Unfortunately, that was not the case. Since my mom was a part of the marital problems, she was a part of the new relationship problems; thus, the fighting continued, just as intense as before. I came to realize that her leaving my father wasn't the answer she always said it would be since he wasn't the entire problem. Ultimately, we found ourselves moving back to Maryland within the year due to legal problems with her boyfriend. I didn't know that when we had left, he had an open arrest warrant; so when he was arrested in Texas, it pinged Maryland authorities. They wanted him back, and my mom and I followed.

Over the next few years, my mom and I still did not become friends. In fact, things got worse, and I moved in with my aunt, then with my older cousin. I watched from a distance as my mom got by and my father did better. Since divorcing, it seemed my mom's problems persisted, were magnified even, and my father's didn't - so who was really the problem when we were growing up? Therapy later taught me that it was, in fact, both of them; that they both still had their individual issues, and one was better supported by society than the other.

With all of this in my past, it's not a surprise I swore off marriage, children and a family for most of my life. Life was certainly not better with a partner; in fact, I had been shown it was much worse. I might go at life alone. Keep friends, have relationships, but ultimately, life was better and more reliable by yourself. So it was a bit of a shock to everyone I knew when I said *"Yes"* to my (now ex-) husband when he proposed on December 13, 2008.

Thirteen years later, we would be recording our divorce.

Prior to our engagement, we shared similar beliefs about marriage. That we were in this until the end and were going to work towards solutions together so that one day we could celebrate 50 years of marriage. Given what I had come from, this may have seemed like a high aspiration. His parents provided a great example of how to work through marriage together...just not the type of marriage I needed or wanted. This was a truth I was not ready or able to see with the young, underdeveloped brain of a 24-year-old. I simply knew I didn't want a marriage like that of my parents, and I didn't want a life that I wanted to escape. So, that was the life we set out to make. I didn't know exactly what I wanted, but I knew what I didn't want. I believed *my* marriage could rescue me from the examples that had been before me.

The first five years of marriage went along well. With minimal responsibilities and dual income, it was easy to live a carefree life with minimal direction. Things began to change for me when we decided to start a family. I began to realize that I wanted more out of life. As I worked to include my new identity of *mother*, I realized I wanted more for me, the family, and our collective future. He was content in the life we had, with little desire to pull more out of the life we lived.

Unknowingly, this was the beginning of our end.

As I began my own self-improvement journey with different life coaches, I could feel him attempt to hold on to me tighter. He would ask me questions about what I was doing in coaching, what the sessions were about, the other women in the cohort...yet he still didn't understand why I was paying for these services. He didn't understand my internal desire (or need) to continually improve. As I delved further into life coaching, I began to consider building my own business. I wanted time, freedom, and the capability to build something I could be truly proud of, not just climb the corporate ladder. As I shared these ideas, his real question came to light: "*Where does this leave me?*"

I remember when he first asked the question; it seemed so odd. After the children had gone to bed, we were sitting around our fire pit on a comfortable fall night, enjoying an adult beverage. I was talking about the possibilities of our future, the benefits of being an entrepreneur, the work required, and how it could affect the family dynamic. Yet, in that moment of my excitement, all he could focus on was how things might affect *him* and the possibility of him being left behind. The question clung to the smoke rising from the fire as I stared at him, confused. I was clearly explaining the potential future roles we would both have to step into and the different freedoms that could come with these changes, yet he couldn't place himself inside the vision.

Interestingly enough, he was so focused on how these potential changes could affect him that he never gave much thought to how *his* actions were affecting *me and the family*. His drinking was a continual point of contention. From our wedding day to that moment, we had had too many discussions, fights, conversations and rules about his drinking, yet things never changed permanently for the better.

In my solo book, *The Break: Rediscovering Our Inner Knowing*, I share how I came to realize that I was so busy existing within co-dependence, I wasn't really living for most of my marriage. I had continued to fulfill the caretaker role I had as a child, except this time it was caretaker of a high-functioning alcoholic. I had entered a marriage without much thought of what I really wanted in life, only what I didn't want, with pieces that were never healed. I had expected marriage and my husband to fix the feelings of loneliness, abandonment, and perfection I silently carried. After the separation and ultimate divorce, when it was only me left, I was able to see that these were parts of my childhood that were carrying me through and keeping me safe. Lovingly, I came to realize that I didn't need to keep holding on to these feelings and their subsequent protective actions anymore. I didn't need someone else to provide security and protection; this was an environment I could create on my own.

The first year of separation, I came back to myself and realized so many times I had ignored my inner knowing, put aside activities I loved and hobbies I wanted to explore, because of parenthood and being married to a high-functioning alcoholic. I realized how weak this had made me and how much of a shell of a person I had become. To hear me say this about myself shocked many, but that didn't make it any less true. My marriage had made me weaker as a person because *I* was unhealthy. My constant need to be *the fixer*, the role I had used as a child in a domestically violent home, was the same role I was playing in my marriage. As a parentified child, I attempted to keep my mom from feeling the pain of her errors; as a wife to a non-violent, non-abusive drunk, I attempted to maintain the persona of perfection. Time, therapy and distance away from my marriage gave me the clarity I didn't have the time to realize before.

I REALIZED I DIDN'T NEED TO BE RESCUED

I needed to heal, to be seen, to enjoy life and to have a stable enough foundation to have the freedom to explore alternate paths forward.

THESE WERE THE GIFTS I HAD TO GIVE TO MYSELF

Three years post-divorce, I continue to gift myself experiences, lessons, dreams, and security.

I love lighthouses. I think they are some of the most unique structures to have existed throughout human history. From the construction to the families that tended them and kept the lights on to guide incoming ships, their existence is magical.

I climbed my first lighthouse in the summer of 2022. It was something I had wanted to do for most of my life and had often said it wasn't possible due to life and family commitments. The excuses were endless. Yet when the "excuses" were no longer present, I had to ask myself why I hadn't gone ahead. Given that I live three hours from the Outer Banks, there was absolutely no reason not to take a day trip and "go climbing."

Since then, I have climbed two more, visited six more, and am planning additional "lighthouse trips" along the East Coast. Some I've visited solo, some other trips have included my children, friends and new love.

By visiting these lighthouses and taking other trips with my children, I am showing them that I am a unique person, more than just their mother. Ten years after having my first child and another child later, I am still becoming more *myself*, and I'm inviting my children along for the journey. They get to watch their mother become a person with endless capabilities, opportunities, and options to create a myriad of futures. They get the freedom to imagine their own future.

No matter the course, their future will be stable, supported, and secured through the actions I had been too timid to enact. Actions I never saw my parents take. I had to explore these actions on my own, mentally, financially, and emotionally. Luckily, I was able to find a great financial advisor and estate attorney to walk me through these processes. Not only did I set up a trust to secure the future of the house we currently live in, but I have also steadily funded their NC 529 accounts on a single income; I've spoken with my daughters about the various steps I have taken to give them security for their future... something my parents were never able to provide me or my brothers. I didn't need large amounts of money to accomplish these processes; I simply needed guidance to know that it was possible.

One of my larger dreams was owning real estate. This was something I used to discuss with my ex while we were married; he never seemed particularly interested in the venture. So I put the idea away in the back of my mind until we were separated. I joined a real estate cohort and began learning different ways to enter the market. One day, the best idea came from one of the leaders- to own a duplex. I started to explore what it would entail to own a duplex and was feeling extremely defeated until I had a conversation about HELOCs and home remodeling. I had to think differently about what I already owned; my house has a basement that had served as a storage unit for over 10 years. It was time to clean it out and re-purpose the space. Again, with the help of my financial advisor, mortgage company, and a great contractor, I've created a 900-square-foot apartment. I've finally entered the real estate market and am looking for ways to expand.

Growing up, I had been shown that security came from others and that I could only have things if other people and systems allowed it to happen; given the circumstances and time in which the women before me had grown up, I'm not surprised this was the mentality they had unknowingly passed down. I had grown up wanting someone to rescue me because that seemed like the only logical response. In reality, I had to put in the work, look myself in the mirror, and rescue myself to create the life I really, truly wanted. Divorce gave me the opportunities and space to see that I am my own heroine.

ABOUT THE AUTHOR

Brandee Melcher is a speaker and an award-winning, best-selling author who balances motherhood, corporate life, travel, and writing. She is on a mission to destigmatize divorce and empower women to choose their best possible futures. Brandee is changing the conversation about co-dependence by acknowledging the truths of the moment *and* the harm experienced with compassion and integrity.

Brandee and her daughters live outside of Raleigh, NC, with their three cats, one dog and a fish.

Connect: Join a community of women that could be an alternative support to Al-Anon: www.skool.com/freda-house-4779

CHAPTER 2

Swept Under the Rug

GROWING UP IN SILENCE

CAROL BRITTON

It was a cold winter night. I remember my mom waking me up, telling me it was time to get dressed for school. I was so confused because it was still dark outside. When I asked her why we were getting up so early, she just told me to hurry, get dressed in my school uniform, and get into the kitchen. When my three brothers (ages 16, 12, and 10), my sister (age 14), and I (age 8) got into the kitchen, we all lined up on the long side of the table. Our dad was sitting at the head of the table ... with a gun and a box of cookies in front of him. I believe the cookies were called Picadilly; they had a coconut, marshmallow, and jam filling. I remember thinking, "He shouldn't be eating cookies right now; it's the middle of the night." Surprisingly, the gun didn't really register with me in that moment. Dad told us all to get out of the house; he said we couldn't take our jackets with us, even though it was the middle of the night during a freezing cold Michigan winter. My older sister defied him by wearing her jacket and taking a blanket. She recently told me that she feared our dad was really going to shoot her in the back as she walked out of the house. We all piled into the car, shivering. We were all cold and scared. My sister shared her coat and blanket with us. Fortunately, my grandmother lived about 20 minutes away, and we went to her house for the night. The only part I remember from being with my grandmother was sitting at the kitchen table and her asking me if I wanted some oatmeal. I have no idea why I remember that. We went home to my dad the next day and never talked about that night again. And when I say never, I mean *never*. It was 2024, 50-plus years after the incident, when my sister shared her terror about potentially being shot.

I share this story because it is the most ingrained memory I have of my father. Of course, there were a few good memories of him – a family vacation or Christmas parties with extended family. But looking back, I never remember my dad being truly present. He usually had a drink in one hand and a cigarette in the other. To him, children were meant to be seen and not heard, and his parenting style was "spare the rod, spoil the child." I did my best to be quiet and stay out of his way.

What I thought was a normal childhood turned out to be anything but. Being the youngest of five, I was sheltered from a lot of goings-on in my household. We didn't talk about divorce, we didn't talk about alcoholism, we didn't talk about abuse – it was our life, and it stayed in our house, and I thought it was normal. Writing this chapter opened the door to conversations with my siblings about our childhood. We have finally lifted the rug and swept out all of the dirt! I was listening to a podcast recently, and they clarified trauma in a way I hadn't heard before. "Big T and Little T" trauma. Big T trauma is things like natural disasters or physical abuse, and little T trauma is relationship problems or job loss. Thinking of trauma in this way made me realize that my mom, my sister, and my brothers all experienced Big T trauma, and yet, we never discussed what was happening under our roof, let alone in terms of being traumatized.

Knowing the trauma my mom experienced and survived makes her one of the strongest and most courageous women I've ever had the privilege to know. As a child, as a difficult teenager or a young adult, I didn't recognize her strength. It wasn't until I had my daughter that I realized what she sacrificed for her five children. In an era when most women were still stay-at-home moms, my mom was a pharmacist. In the early 1970s, 10% of pharmacists in the United States were women; my mom was one of them. She was also the wife of an abusive alcoholic, a mother of five, lived in an affluent suburb of Detroit, and was a Catholic.

My dad was also a pharmacist, which is a bad career for someone who was also an alcoholic. The memories I have of my father are not good. My siblings may have a different perspective, but to me, my father was evil. My memories of him consist of being kicked out of the house at gunpoint, being paddled with a wooden cutting board, and seeing pictures of the new baby he had with another woman all over his pharmacy before my parents were divorced.

My father owned his own drugstore as we were growing up, so he worked 12-hour days, seven days a week. He was so busy trying to "keep up with the Joneses." He drove a Cadillac, lived in an affluent community, had 5 kids in private school, etc., but this was not sustainable. So, while he worked hard, he took his anger and frustration out on his family.

It was in the early 1970s, shortly after he kicked us out of the house at gunpoint, when my parents split; I was 8 years old, and my oldest brother was 16. Being Catholic meant that my mom was excommunicated, shunned by most of her "closest friends," and left to raise five children on her own. This was a time when being a single mother was stigmatized and carried an air of shame along with it. There were no support networks for single parents, and she was mostly left to fend for herself. She had two very close and loyal friends who were always there for her. Looking back, I can now see that even a little support helped her carry a heavy load. I was 8 years old at the time and thought this was just what moms did. They provided for their family, regardless of the cost. I had no idea of the struggles and turmoil my mom was going through to keep a roof over our heads. She sacrificed everything for us.

After the divorce was final, my dad rarely provided child support, never sent birthday or Christmas cards. I never heard from him again. I only recently learned my mom had a restraining order out for my dad, which could explain some of his absence. He eventually gave up on trying to be part of our lives because my mom made it hard for him to see us. I can't blame her for this because of the abuse we all suffered at his hands.

My mom had to go back to work full-time at a local pharmacy and usually came home exhausted. This meant my brothers, sister, and I were left to take care of the household. We were expected to do our chores, finish homework, and look out for each other. And we were told that what happened inside the house stayed inside the house. Which meant I couldn't talk to my friends; we certainly didn't talk about it inside the house. So, while my mom and dad both instilled a great work ethic in me, the ability to have a frank and honest discussion was not something we did. My mom was the queen of "sweep it under the rug and it will go away."

In my teenage years, having a lack of supervision because my mom was working to raise five kids, I started to get into a lot of trouble. I did not make the best choices in friends or boyfriends. Most of my friends were from very well-to-do families, and they had access to things that I normally wouldn't have had because I didn't have the money. However, they taught me how to drink and attend parties; when I look back, I'm surprised I survived. My mom was never one to have a confrontation with you; again, she liked to sweep everything under the rug. She would give you the "look," lay a good dose of Catholic guilt upon you, and find a way to express her disappointment in your choice. For example, I used to smoke in high school. She was not happy with this decision, so to let me know how she felt, she would take my cigarettes out of my purse, run the pack under water, get them nice and wet, and then put them back in my purse without ever saying a word. When I would leave the house and grab a cigarette from my pack of smokes, I would find them ruined. This was her way of letting me know that she knew I smoked and was extremely disappointed in the decision that I had made. At that point in my life, all it did was make me angry with her because I had to go out of my way to the store and spend more money on cigarettes.

Looking back, I know she didn't have the energy to confront me on things like smoking and drinking. After all, I was one of five children she was raising while working full-time. She cared deeply for all of us, always pushing us to do our best and be our best, always teaching us how to make it on our own, telling us we had to be able to live on our own and support ourselves before we got married. Spouses, she told me, must be partners, supporting and helping each other, not a person you rely on for your very existence. I never thought about money as a child as we didn't go without. We lived in an affluent community. As I got older, it became more apparent that my mom was struggling to make ends meet. She could stretch a can of pork-n-beans and a package of hot dogs into a glorious batch of "beanie weenies" that everyone enjoyed.

Her second husband, whom we will call "Joe," was a true miser. When I say, "true miser," I mean it. Once, Mom, Joe, one of my brothers, and I took a trip to Toronto when I was around 12 years old. We were going out to dinner and ended up driving around until after 6:00 p.m. so that he didn't have to put money in a parking meter. We had a nice meal, but took the leftover bread with us so that we could eat it for breakfast the next morning. While I appreciate the value of a dollar, eating stale bread for breakfast while on vacation was not my idea of a good time. But he did know how to manage money, and that was something my mom needed at that point in time. The marriage didn't last long, fortunately, but it helped my mom get her financial footing.

One of the earliest "life lessons" I remember her teaching me and my siblings was how to shake hands and look someone in the eye while introducing ourselves. At family parties, we would get paid a nickel for every hand we shook while looking the person in the eye and asking them, "How do you do?" Little did I know, this would be a critical skill in advancing my career, as I was able to portray a calm, confident demeanor, even if I was nervous inside. First impressions are lasting impressions. Having the ability to go into an interview with a confident handshake was one of the most useful tools to me in my career. Not only did it help set the tone of the interview, but helped calm my nerves every single time.

Another thing she taught us throughout our childhood was the importance of being on time. When the church bell rang at 6, you had better be in your seat at the dinner table. As a child, I thought this was just because dinner was ready. However, she did this for several reasons. Yes, dinner was ready, but there was more to it. She worked hard to put food on the table, and she was teaching us to appreciate her effort by being respectful and showing up on time (with our hands already washed.) It was also a time where we talked about our day, and she could lay eyes on us and make sure we were ok. Wrangling 5 kids, making sure they were fed, healthy, and not bleeding too badly (we came home with skinned knees and elbows daily) is a large load for a single parent. This was before cell phones and video games. We played outside all day, came home for lunch or had lunch at a friend's, back out to play, home for dinner (on time,) chores, then back out to play until the streetlights came on. When the streetlights come on, you'd better be running for home. This was her way of teaching us to be respectful of everyone's time – if you're 5 minutes early, you're late.

Other things that were important to my mother were playing a musical instrument, playing a sport, and doing well in school. Hard work and discipline in a task were her mode of parenting, not discipline with a paddle.

All my siblings learned to read music at an early age. I started with piano at home, then learned flute in elementary school to join the band. I played until I started high school, when being a member of the band was not "cool," so I gave up the flute and joined the choir. Music was important to my mom, so when she married her third and final husband, "John," I wasn't surprised that he too, enjoyed music. He sang in a barbershop quartet, which at the time I thought was rather dull, but my mom loved hearing him sing.

By this time, I was the last child to go to college, and was glad my mom had someone by her side. When it came time for college, it wasn't a question of "if" we were going, but where we were going and how we would pay for it. I opted to attend Michigan State University, where I could get in-state tuition; besides, many of my friends were heading there. When I started college, I knew I was going to be a Certified Public Accountant. Well, that quickly changed my junior year when I took tax classes and knew I couldn't do that the rest of my life. I decided to change majors, but had to make the hard call home to tell my mom. I was dreading the call because I thought I would disappoint her. I still remember to this day calling my mom while lying in my bed, clutching a pillow, ready to hear her disappointment in my choice. However, she assured me it was OK, and asked if I had given any thought as to what I might like to do. She also encouraged me to stay a business major so I wouldn't lose all the credits I had already earned. A sense of relief and calm quickly washed over me, and we chatted about the many possible majors I could pursue. Education was so important to my mother. She wanted to ensure we could support ourselves, so having a long conversation about my future shouldn't have been a surprise. I ended up changing my major a couple of times and graduated with a degree in Supply Chain Management. This turned out to be the best decision of my life. It led me to my husband (now married 30+ years,) my amazing daughter, my wonderful stepson, and a rich and rewarding career.

With "John" by her side, my mom finally seemed to relax and enjoy life. She and "John" travelled often, played golf, and the house was always full of music. They were married for over 30 years and were great role models on how to treat each other with respect and kindness.

While I didn't see it as a child, teenager, or young adult, looking back, my mom showed her love by working hard, preparing us to face the future and to become strong, independent people. The struggles and trauma my siblings and I faced created a special bond.

It's interesting to me that my three brothers reconciled with our father later in life while my sister and I never forgave him. My brothers were in their 40s and 50s when they reached out to him at different points in time. What they shared with me was that he was very mild-mannered and had been married to his current wife for over 30 years. She was the same woman with whom he had an affair while married to our mother.

I understand why they chose to forgive him, but for me, the past is not easily swept under the rug. No matter how tired or frustrated he was, nothing justifies the verbal and physical abuse we endured. He made choices, to live beyond his means, to drown his anger in alcohol, to turn it on his family, and we bore the brunt of them. Forgiveness, I've learned, is deeply personal. My brothers found peace in it. My sister and I found peace without it.

Because of, or perhaps despite of, our traumatic upbringing, my siblings and I carry an unbreakable bond. We live miles and countries apart, but we are always there for each other when it matters. Some of them have faced divorces, others have been in long, happy marriages. We have all built successful careers, raised wonderful children, and are living lives filled with joy.

In the end, our childhood taught us two things: conversations need to happen, don't sweep it under the rug, and have the strength to stand on your own. The silence that once defined our home no longer defines us. Instead, we are bound together by the understanding of what we survived, and the life we built beyond it.

ABOUT THE AUTHOR

Carol Britton, a survivor of a challenging childhood marked by silence and trauma, has used her experiences to build a life full of love and success.

Growing up as the youngest of five in a household dealing with alcoholism and abuse, she learned the importance of resilience, hard work, and the transformative power of open conversation.

Despite a challenging upbringing, she and her siblings forged an unbreakable bond, charting their individual paths to successful careers, fulfilling relationships, and full lives. Her journey highlights the deeply personal nature of forgiveness and the strength that comes from confronting the past rather than sweeping it under the rug.

Through her writing, she advocates for open and honest dialogue, celebrating the strength that comes from overcoming adversity.

Connect:
www.linkedin.com/in/carol-britton-47a2257
www.instagram.com/cabritton441
www.facebook.com/carol.britton.355

CHAPTER 3
Finding My True Self in the Splits
LESLEY GOTH, PSYD

When I think about writing a chapter for a book called *Split*, I can't help but chuckle. Of course, I have a story to share! After all, I've been married and divorced twice. As a psychologist, I spend my days helping couples navigate the complexities of love, communication, and connection.

I want to delve into a journey that extends beyond the dissolution of unhappy marriages; it encompasses my profound separation from another deeply traumatic relationship—my connection to a Christian church. A cult, to be precise.

Letting go of any toxic or unhealthy relationship is a challenging, yet essential, step toward reclaiming one's true self. It's necessary to acknowledge that it's perfectly acceptable to "see the light" and make the courageous decision to break free, even in the face of overwhelming shame, blame, and condemnation. This chapter is about embracing that empowerment and the transformative path that follows.

So, let's embark on this journey together. Let's explore generational trauma, the pitfalls of attaching to the wrong people, the transformative power of self-love and joy, and the profound process of spiritual healing that allows us to reclaim our authentic selves.

THE EARLY YEARS

I remember wishing my parents would get divorced. Their relationship felt cold and distant, and family gatherings often left me feeling more like a spectator than a participant. My dad was the scrupulous protector, my mom was nurturing yet permissive. As a teenager, I longed for freedom; I thought their divorce might be my ticket out.

When I was 15, my dad confided in me about unhappiness in his marriage and his thoughts of leaving my mom. I encouraged him to pursue happiness, saying life is too short to be miserable. His surprised and proud reaction, along with his suggestion that I consider becoming a psychologist due to my "mature" response, inspired me, planting the seed for my future career.

At the time, I thought my overprotective father's moving out would mean I was gaining freedom. The aftermath of that conversation was far from what I expected. My mom fell into a deep depression, struggling to get out of bed and take care of herself. I needed her more than ever, but she grieved deeply, understandably so. I was a good student and dedicated dancer, but in my confusion, I turned to partying, trying to fill the empty void. I was also starving myself and drowning my pain in drugs and alcohol. My mom and I were both lost, navigating separate paths of despair.

I remember my mom confiding that she realized she was making a mistake the day she married my dad. It explained some things but left me questioning why anyone would marry without being in love, especially since she was not pregnant or "needing" to get married for any other reason.

THE IMPACT OF MY PARENTS' DIVORCE

Looking back, I admit I was relieved when my parents divorced. They were mismatched in so many ways—my dad craved social interaction and excitement, my mom preferred the tranquility of home and nature. Their struggles to support each other's passions highlighted their incompatibility. However, I was floundering, caught between the freedom I craved and the pain I suppressed. I felt torn, wanting to support my mom while also seeking my dad's approval. It was a no-win situation, and I often felt like I was betraying both parents.

The impact of divorce on children is profound, regardless of age. It's hard to navigate the emotional landscape of a split family, often feeling the pressure to choose sides. Yet, suppose parents can remain healthy and amicable. In that case, children can adapt more easily and understand that their parents' happiness apart can be beneficial for everyone involved.

Eventually, my mom found her wings and began to thrive. But my parents planted seeds I was not even aware of at the time.

GENERATIONAL CYCLES CONTINUE

Fast forward to my first marriage. Like my mom before me, I knew I shouldn't be marrying this man. He was a good man, but he lacked the emotional attunement and support I needed. I aspired to a particular lifestyle, influenced by my father's emphasis on financial security. I thought my first husband could provide that for me.

We had two exceptional children, whom I cherish and adore. But after 17 years of marriage, when my daughter turned 15—the same age I was when my dad left—and my son was 12, I realized our relationship lacked the depth I hungered for. Despite our efforts in couples counseling, I was unhappy. The Christian guilt weighed heavily on me; there was no infidelity or clear justification for ending a marriage. I battled the belief that pursuing my own happiness would be selfish and destructive to my family.

At the time our marriage was unraveling, my ex-husband and I were members of a small church that we had helped establish. We loved and trusted the pastor and believed in his vision. We poured our hearts into its foundation, and I was able to offer support and counseling to those who attended. In that community, I felt a profound sense of belonging —something truly special and unique. Sadly, not something I had ever really felt before. In addition, there was an emotional depth lacking in my marriage that my church relationships richly fulfilled.

SEEKING PERMISSION—ANOTHER CYCLE REPEATS ITSELF

In a moment of irony, I had a conversation with my dad, who, after all those years, gave me the same advice I had given him–that life was too short to be miserable. It was a lightbulb moment. I realized I was allowed to seek my own joy, but I still needed to wait for the right timing. It was a profound moment I will never forget when God spoke to me, revealing that my husband would never change and that it was okay to end things. The burden of maintaining a false relationship lifted, and I felt empowered to pursue a life filled with genuine connection and joy.

LEAVING FOR THE RIGHT REASONS

These revelations are not to imply that I was not suffering. I found myself engulfed in a whirlwind of conflicting emotions, particularly during the period following my decision to end my marriage. On one hand, I felt an overwhelming sense of guilt and shame for choosing to leave a relationship that had been a significant part of my life for nearly two decades. I worried about the impact my decision would have on my children, fearing that I was shattering their sense of stability and security. The weight of these feelings often left me paralyzed, questioning whether I was genuinely doing the right thing.

Amidst the chaos, a small spark of certainty emerged, reassuring me that I was making the right decision for my own well-being. I recognized that remaining in a situation where I felt trapped and unfulfilled was not a viable option. I yearned for happiness and a sense of purpose, yet anxiety and fear overshadowed my journey. The daunting reality of becoming financially independent weighed heavily on me, as I struggled with a profound lack of confidence in my ability to navigate life on my own without a partner. The idea of taking full responsibility for my future was both exhilarating and terrifying.

Once officially on my own, I turned to various distractions. I immersed myself in a range of mind-numbing activities—dating excessively, socializing with friends, and drinking. While these temporary diversions offered brief moments of relief, they ultimately left me feeling emptier and more alienated. I was seeking happiness in inappropriate places, attempting to fill an emotional void without engaging in the essential inner work required for genuine healing.

I came to understand that although I was enthusiastic about starting a new phase in my life, I still bore the burden of unresolved emotions. Instead of confronting my feelings, I attempted to evade them, convinced that staying numb and busy would eventually lead me to the happiness I desired. However, I was miserable.

It was in this misery that I realized it was time to confront my feelings of guilt, shame, and fear. By facing these emotions head-on, I could clear a path toward a more promising future—one where I could embrace my autonomy and discover joy according to my own standards.

Keep in mind that as my marriage was coming to an end, the situation within the church began to deteriorate as well. I became increasingly aware of unsettling issues that raised concerns for me. Inappropriate sexual relationships were emerging, there were indications of excessive control, coercion, and manipulation over the congregation, and members faced pressure to participate and live their lives in particular ways. The teachings started to feel misaligned with my spiritual beliefs, focusing more on personal agendas, rather than genuinely reflecting God's heart. Ultimately, an ever-so-subtle evolution of control and manipulation became evident, leading to a literal split within the entire church.

It's challenging to separate from a church, particularly when faced with accusations of opposing God's will, being accused of "living in sin" and "according to my flesh." The pastor told me I was leading others astray. The guilt and manipulation were tangible. It is devastating—and disorienting—when those you have trusted suddenly label you as walking with Satan. I needed to distance myself to reflect independently on my beliefs, determine what felt genuine regarding my relationship with God, and whether I would ever attend another church or open my Bible again. This process was arduous, especially amidst the dissolution of my family.

So, now I found myself not only confronting the stigma associated with divorce but also dealing with the disgrace of having been part of a cult. I couldn't shake off my concern about how others might perceive me, an educated woman who had been misled and manipulated in such a manner.

Approximately 8 months after my divorce and leaving the church, I met my second husband. I recognized that I was making an error in judgment once again. It felt as though I had become too entrenched in the relationship to extricate myself. I had yet to develop the confidence necessary to meet my own needs independently. Often, I perceived myself as more of an object for use, rather than as someone deserving of care and appreciation.

After a European vacation together, where I felt little to no connection, no friendship, no compatibility, no nothing, I knew it was time to split. I realized that I could no longer rely on external validation or relationships to define my happiness. I embarked on a path of self-discovery and healing, confronting the demons that had deviled me for so long. This process was not easy; it required immense courage to face the pain and trauma I had buried deep within. But as I delved into the depths of my emotions, I began to free myself from the chains of my past.

Through therapy, self-reflection, and a commitment to nurturing my well-being, I gradually learned to love and care for myself without needing a man to complete me. I discovered the importance of building a healthy relationship with my body and food, recognizing that my worth and others' perception of me are not tied together. This journey of self-acceptance and empowerment was transformative, allowing me to reclaim my identity and embrace the life I truly desired. There was no question that God played the most pivotal role in this healing journey.

Looking back, I see that the years spent navigating through confusion and regret were essential to my growth. They taught me invaluable lessons about resilience, self-love, and the importance of going as deeply as possible to heal truly.

What I finally learned, albeit slowly, was that I could provide for myself. I didn't need financial security; I needed warmth and emotional support. I needed someone who truly saw me, loved me for who I was, and not just for my appearance. This realization marked a turning point in my life. It took me many years to truly understand how I could not only survive but thrive.

HOW DID I HEAL FOR REAL?

I had to confront and crush my perfectionism. I was able to achieve this by learning how to truly love myself and allowing self-compassion to become my life's driving force. For so long, I had been trapped in a cycle of unrealistic expectations, constantly striving for an unattainable ideal that left me feeling inadequate and exhausted. Aiming for the perfect body, relationship, career, and so on, had become a shield, protecting me from vulnerability but also isolating me from genuine connection and joy. I also needed to process childhood trauma that was a significant factor in my unhealthy relationships with food, my body, and men!

1. I got back into therapy, validating that therapists need therapy too! Though I had done considerable work on myself, and all of it was valuable, nothing compared to the breakthroughs I experienced at this low point in my life.
2. EMDR (Eye Movement Desensitization and Reprocessing) helped me uncover the deepest wounds and negative messages I had carried with me for so long. It was as if I was peeling back layers of buried pain from deep within, allowing me to confront and process experiences that I had previously avoided. The gentle yet powerful nature of EMDR enabled me to reframe my past, transforming the way I viewed my trauma and its impact on my life.
3. Through intentional breathing techniques, I was able to access locked-away feelings, allowing me to express and release emotions that I had suppressed for years. This practice not only helped me connect with my body but also facilitated a profound sense of clarity and peace. It was the most significant release of pain I had ever experienced.
4. I had to embark on a journey of understanding my own faith and what it truly meant to me to be a Christian and a follower of Jesus. For much of my adult life, I learned within a framework of legalistic structures that did not resonate with my true sense of self or align with my heart's desires. These rigid interpretations of faith left me feeling

constrained and disconnected from the essence of my true beliefs.

I realized that my faith had to be rooted in love—first, in loving God wholeheartedly, and then in allowing His love to flow through me to others. It had nothing to do with what church I attended or how many hours I read my Bible. This revelation changed me. Shifting my perspective from one of obligation and fear to one of grace and compassion. I began to understand that loving others with the same grace and compassion that God extends to me every single day was not just a calling, but a beautiful expression of my faith.

FROM SPLIT TO WHOLE

I have never felt freer or more filled with joy. Embracing my authentic self has been a transformative experience, allowing me to step into a life that feels true to who I am. I've cultivated a sense of independence that empowers me, yet I also cherish the deep connections I've formed with others. These relationships are life-giving, enriching my existence rather than draining my energy.

What I like most about myself is the profound sense of freedom I feel in being myself. I've liberated myself from the need for others' approval. I now make choices that align with my true nature, rather than conforming to what others expect me to be or wish I were. This shift has allowed me to embrace my individuality and celebrate the unique qualities that make me who I am.

As a result, there is very little room left for perfectionism or shame in my mind and body. While those feelings may occasionally resurface, I've developed the tools and resilience to recognize them for what they are—temporary distractions rather than definitions. I've learned how to squash those negative thoughts and continue living freely, focusing on self-acceptance and compassion.

EXTREME GRATITUDE

I am definitely grateful for my two divorces. I am equally thankful for the religious trauma I endured while in the cult. Both were challenging experiences, but the wisdom and insights I gained from them are invaluable. Through these journeys, I have learned critical lessons about resilience, self-worth, and the pursuit of happiness. I have taught my children the strength to pursue their own peace and joy, even when it means making difficult decisions.

It took navigating early life confusion about marriage and relationships, processing my traumas, discovering my true self, establishing my faith based on freedom and love, and having the courage never to settle until I found what I truly wanted. I learned to pursue and embrace my joy and peace. It pains me to see friends or clients who are miserable in their relationships, feeling trapped by circumstances. I want to empathize with their struggles while emphasizing the importance of finding a partner who loves you for who you are.

The best outcomes of these splits and all the personal work I have done are twofold. First and foremost, I have developed an awareness and relationship with myself that I base on love, compassion, and self-care. The perfectionist in me has quieted down, released control, and learned to trust my intuition.

The second is the profound connections I can now establish with my clients. My experiences have equipped me with a unique perspective that goes beyond just addressing relationship struggles. I understand that many of the challenges they face are rooted in deeper issues—traumas that have not been processed and continue to manifest in their lives.

The journey to self-discovery is powerful. The more you heal your wounds, quiet the voices that have led you astray, the more empowered you become. There is immense power in self-love and self-discovery. You deserve to be seen, heard, known, and loved. So go ahead—embrace your journey.

Embrace your splits.

ABOUT THE AUTHOR

Lesley Goth, Psyd, is an award-winning, best-selling author and licensed clinical psychologist with over 21 years of experience in private practice, dedicated to supporting individuals on their journey to healing and recovery. As an author and public speaker, Lesley is passionate about sharing knowledge and insights that empower others, particularly those who have experienced trauma. Her work primarily focuses on helping sexual assault survivors navigate the complexities of their healing journey, utilizing Eye Movement Desensitization and Reprocessing (EMDR) therapy as a transformative tool for recovery.

Through Lesley's practice, writing, and speaking, she strives to create a safe and compassionate space where clients can explore their experiences, reclaim their narratives, and foster resilience. Lesley believes in the profound healing capacity within each person and is committed to guiding them toward a brighter, more hopeful future.

Connect:
  TikTok: @traumahealer
  IG: @tramahealer11
  Facebook: www.facebook.com/Denverfamilycounselingservices
  LinkedIn: www.linkedin.com/in/denverfamilycounseling
  Website: www.denverfamilycounselingservices.com

CHAPTER 4

There Is No Such Thing as a Normal Family

CAROLINA CIFUENTES

I guess it is never easy for anyone to have a conversation about something as painful—and often definitive—as a separation. This story is not just about me; it is for everyone who has ever felt their life and their world falling apart, and who had to become a whole new person just to make it through what was required of them.

My name is Carolina, and I am a child of divorce, raised in a broken migrant home. I was born in Colombia, in a simple and frugal household. My parents married when they were very young: she was nineteen, and he was twenty-eight. At that age, most of us barely know who we are or what the world is about. But life has a way of teaching the lessons we need by placing us in the exact circumstances where those lessons unfold. I came into their lives just two years after their paths joined. The year was 1989.

When I was a child, our family was very poor. My grandparents worked as caretakers of a finca—a large country house that did not belong to them, but one that they looked after, cleaning, gardening, keeping everything in order. Because my parents couldn't afford a place of their own, we were allowed to live in a single room there. During the week, my dad worked in the countryside, and I would only see him on weekends, when he came home to rest. My mom spent her days helping my grandma with the work of the finca, while I wandered through the meadows like a forest fairy. Even from a very young age, I could feel my family living separate lives: my dad away most of the time, my mom absorbed by her duties, and me left to my own world in nature. Strangely enough, those were also the happiest and freest years of my life. In retrospect, I now see that my family was *split* in many ways throughout my life—sometimes by circumstance, sometimes by choice, and sometimes by silence.

By the time I was five, my dad had enough financial stability to provide for a home. So, we left the countryside and my beloved finca, and found a small apartment in a little town. For me, this was a big change: I used to be free, able to run around the trees. Now, I was expected to be confined to a one-bedroom apartment, not allowed to spend much time outside, as we did not live in a safe area.

My dad, who always carried the best intentions for our family, especially in terms of financial security, realized how little we had and made a decision that would forever change our paths: he decided to migrate. I was about eight when this happened. My mom and I moved into my uncle's home while my dad traveled to Switzerland with the hope of building a better future for all of us. My family was once again separated.

Even though he was away, he was always my hero—going into battle alone so we could have a better chance at life. I was only eight, but I believed he was out there conquering new lands for us. That belief made the emptiness of his absence a little easier to bear, knowing that each day apart was carrying us closer to those faraway Swiss lands where our paths would meet again.

Being reunited in Switzerland felt like a dream, almost like stepping into a fantasy. After years of having just enough to cover the basics, suddenly we had a countryside home in the Alps provided by the government. I would later learn that my father had applied for political asylum as a way to migrate, but at the time, that detail did not mean much to me. What mattered was that we were together again, that once more, I was free to wander through the meadows. The meadows were more than grass and flowers; they meant freedom, a space where I could just be. I had known that joy before, back in the Colombian countryside of my earliest years; being able to feel it again in Switzerland made it seem as though heaven had opened for me.

But that heaven was short-lived. We could not stay for more than a year. When you migrate under political asylum, many of your decisions are no longer your own—they belong to the government. Once officials reassessed our case, they ruled our lives were not under threat, and the government decided it was safe for us to return to Colombia. Our passports were taken, and we received them back only as we boarded the plane to leave the country. Returning to Colombia was no longer a choice; it was the only option left to us.

When we came back, my mom got pregnant. The news came as a surprise to all of us, but there was more worry than joy. If there was barely enough for three, how was my dad supposed to provide for four? The financial burden felt heavy on his shoulders, and even though he rarely voiced it, the weight was visible in the way he carried himself. My mom had always been the type of person who kept her emotions and thoughts to herself, but I could sense the tension in her silence. I could tell that this new pregnancy meant her ties to my dad would extend…whether she wanted them to or not.

There are times when we would rather stay silent than voice our concerns. Fear convinces us that speaking out will only make things harder to bear. And so we choose quiet, believing it will protect us. But the more we feed the silence, the more the problems grow.

My mom had married as a way of escaping her family home, not because she had fallen in love. Without education or a path to provide for herself, finding a husband felt like her only way out. But the choice was born out of necessity rather than desire. She had stepped into a life that offered survival but not freedom. Now, with another child on the way, both she and my dad were facing a situation neither of them was ready to take on. In many ways, my mother's silence began long before that pregnancy; it began the day she chose survival over freedom.

My parents were confused, worried, and scared… and then, in the middle of an impossible situation, they came to me for advice. I remember the moment clearly when my mom asked me whether I wanted a sibling or not. I was only a child, but I understood instantly what that question meant. They were considering not moving forward, and by asking me, they were trying to ease the weight on their conscience, to hear from the one person whose honesty they trusted most.

They knew I would not lie. They knew my heart would lean toward what was right, even if it meant more hardship for us all. And so I answered with the only truth I had: that I would love to have a little brother or sister, and that nothing would make me happier than to welcome a new life into our family. I said it with the innocence of a child who believed love could soften any burden. But behind my words was also a quiet conviction—that even in struggle, choosing life was the only choice we could live with.

It was only in my thirties that I came to understand how that conversation had shaped my identity for the rest of my life. I was a child making an adult's decision, and from that moment on, something inside me stepped into adulthood. As a little girl, I had no hesitation; I could hear my heart clearly and speak my truth, no matter the consequences. It is a skill we are all born with, but one we often forget as we grow older. That was also the moment I realized how hard the world could be. It took me many years, many mistakes, to recover trust—in the world, in my heart, in my intuition—and to finally feel safe speaking my truth again.

My parents decided to listen to me, and we moved on. We would never speak of that conversation again, at least not openly. Then, just a few weeks later, came another surprise. During my mom's first ultrasound, the doctor congratulated her—the monitor showed not one, but two heartbeats. Two lives were coming instead of one. My mom began to cry, and in her tears, I could sense both the beauty of the moment and the weight of guilt she carried from her initial hesitation; that mix of joy and sorrow has stayed with her ever since.

That moment wasn't just about my mother—it was about what society was expecting from her, from women everywhere. The world expects so much of us. We are expected to obey, to provide, to care, to nurture... but who nurtures us when something like this happens? When we carry something we cannot speak of openly, something so brutal it can fracture us from the inside? These are the kinds of wounds that don't show on the surface, wounds that shape everything that comes after. My family was never the same after this moment. It was as if each of us silently picked up a role—not chosen freely, but assigned by circumstance—so that we could survive and keep moving forward. And in doing so, we learned to carry on. But not without cost. The silence became part of our story, like a ghost present in rooms where no words were spoken.

I have no idea how our lives would have unfolded if we had decided differently. These kinds of decisions are never easy, and whether or not you've faced an impossible situation and made a choice that has stayed with you forever, I want you to know this: only by looking back and embracing what was, we can find peace in the now.

Given the new landscape and our new roles, we all had to make decisions and adjust accordingly. My dad had not expected to start over raising children at forty, and he took on that burden with a lot of resistance; my mother chose to dedicate her time and energy to the newborns as a way to quiet her conscience and make peace with the decision she had once considered. And I became the unbreakable kid—the support my parents could count on. I was the one who always had to look strong and composed so they wouldn't have to worry about me, the one who could handle whatever was needed. I knew the load they carried was already heavy, and I didn't want to add more weight to it. In learning to carry the weight for everyone else, I forgot that I, too, was just a child in need of being carried.

My dad found a way to migrate once more; he packed his dreams and fears and went to Spain. Four years would pass before we were reunited again, this time in Colombia—a reunion that exposed everything that was already broken. My brothers didn't know their father, as he had been away during their first years. My dad didn't know how to build a loving and patient relationship with them. My mom realized that the only reason she remained was the children, and the belief that our only chance at a better future would come if we eventually moved to Spain. And I was in my teens, barely understanding the dynamics unfolding around me, yet doing my best to avoid what felt inevitable. We all moved to Spain shortly after, in quiet acceptance of the roles we had taken on.

There is an idea that having a united home will do more good than harm; I could not disagree more. Many times, couples decide to stay in a marriage believing it is for the well-being of their children. But a home without love, compassion, and open communication is simply not a home. It is a prison you are not allowed to leave, and the time you spend there leaves lasting marks on everyone who endures it.

In such a prison, there is anger, sadness, frustration, fear, resentment, guilt, resignation, countless other emotions and dynamics that silently shape who you become and how you relate to the outside world. More unconsciously than consciously, I fled from that situation as soon as I could. When I left my family home, I did not just change cities—I needed real distance, and so I moved to another country. It was one of the hardest decisions of my life. I knew I would finally be free, but I also knew my brothers would be left alone. I had been the only person in that family they could truly talk to and rely on, the only one who allowed them to just be kids. Leaving gave me freedom, but it also left a wound between us. Our relationship was never the same after I left.

My mother finally decided to end things when my brothers were twenty-one years old. She felt it was a safe age to leave her marriage, trusting that her sons already had the skills and knowledge to continue with their lives. By then, she also had a job and savings, which meant she could look after herself financially. This is one of the main reasons many women don't leave earlier—they fear they won't be able to survive without their partner's support. My father, however, was not expecting this news. In his eyes, we were a normal family, and nothing was wrong at home.

For me, the decision felt long overdue. At first, I was relieved to know it was finally happening. But as time passed, a sense of dread began to grow in me. Even though I was living abroad, I had always carried the idea of a home, a structure I could rely on, a place I could return to whenever life got rough. It was as if I had been a peninsula, still tied in some way to the continent called family. But then an earthquake came, severing that connection to the mainland, and I was left as a stranded island that no longer belonged anywhere. Knowing something should happen, then living it and feeling all its consequences are two very different things.

Suddenly, the *split* was real, and I felt as if my home and the very foundations of my life had disappeared. How was *normal* life supposed to look moving forward? What would happen to birthdays? How would we celebrate Christmas? What about my wedding day—could both of my parents be there, and be civil to one another? These are questions I still don't have answers for. But I do hold hope for creating happier memories—and I know that, at least in part, it depends on me.

Beyond being a family and a societal construct, we are all human beings, each of us having our own experience of this thing called life. We are all growing, learning, and evolving as we go. The years spent in a home where no one truly wanted to be will never come back. And even though we all emerged with scars, those scars shaped the humans we are today. Parents often delay the decision to separate, believing it is in the best interest of the children. They fail to see the consequences of staying. They think that because there is no physical violence, we -the children- don't notice when things are off. That we don't hear the silence, the cold looks, the misplaced comments. But we notice everything. And we learn, in turn, to remain silent ourselves, to find ways to cope with what is left unspoken. Listening to what children have to say could give parents a very different perspective on what is truly 'best for them.' As kids, we don't ask for perfection—we just want to be loved, heard, understood, and to know that our voices matter.

There is a phrase in *A Return to Love* by Marianne Williamson that says, 'A miracle is just a shift in perception.' That is exactly what has happened to me and the way I see everything that took place—and even what never did. I stopped judging my parents and their decisions. I came to understand that the greatest gift they ever gave me was life, and the lives of my brothers. But not only that: they went beyond themselves and their personal preferences to keep us well, nourished, and safe, to give us the best they could so that we might access opportunities they themselves were never allowed to dream of. My parents are my heroes, and I owe them my gratitude and devotion. They have done way more than enough.

Looking back now, I see that what my parents gave me was never perfect, but it was real. Love and care were always there, in their own imperfect way—and that is the gift I choose to carry forward.

My family is not *normal*. It never has been, and it never will be. But what does a *normal family* even mean? Who decided what a family should look like, or how it should live? Culture? Tradition? Religion? Marketing? The truth is, the idea of a *normal family* has no real foundation. Families come in all shapes and forms, none better than another—each different, each unique in its own way. Perhaps the greatest freedom comes when we stop longing for *normal*, and instead choose to see the beauty right in front of us: the family we have, and the love we are brave enough to give—and to receive. For me, the way forward is in not chasing an idea of normality, but in loving, accepting, and embracing the family I have—exactly as it is.

ABOUT THE AUTHOR

Carolina Cifuentes is an economist, holistic therapist, writer, and international speaker. With a background that bridges economics, integrative health, and family constellations, she guides leaders and individuals in high-stress environments to reclaim their energy, health, productivity, and well-being. Her philosophy is simple yet profound: *"cuidarte es honrar tu propósito"*—to care for yourself is to honor your purpose.

Through her integrative approach—combining systemic awareness, emotional healing, and practical strategies—Carolina helps both people and organizations uncover the hidden dynamics that shape relationships, leadership, and performance. She believes that when we heal within, we create companies and communities that are more sustainable, conscious, and human-centered.

As a contributing writer in *Split*, she expands her voice to a global audience. Her vision is to continue inspiring transformation as an international speaker and collaborator, building bridges between well-being, leadership, and innovation worldwide.

Connect:
www.carovitalidad.com
www.linkedin.com/in/carocifuentes
www.instagram.com/caro_vitalidad

CHAPTER 5
The Radical Reframe
SEPARATION AS SUCCESS

SIERRA MELCHER

"Congratulations!"

What if that was a normal response to the news of a break-up? Can you even imagine?

I have taken to asking, *"And how do you feel about that?"* when I hear anyone say *"I got divorced,"* or *"We separated."* Rather than assuming the common imposition of cultural narrative: *"Oh, I am so sorry."*

What if it is a good thing, or better than the alternative? Mine was. Many are. We wouldn't separate if being together was better, now would we?

Every separation is unique, yet they share some common elements. What makes mine worth sharing isn't the drama or the heartbreak; it's the radical reframe I've had to undergo as both the child of separated parents and now a single mother myself, living in Colombia, navigating between Latino and gringo expectations about family, men, solo parenting, and what constitutes success.

I am not going to relitigate the separation from my daughter's father here. It doesn't feel fair to her to do so in the pages of this book. But I *will* challenge every assumption you might have about what my story means, what it cost, and what it gave us both.

THE CULTURAL SCRIPT WE'RE HANDED

"Staying together for the children."

It might sound quaint, but this is still a heavy cultural burden and assumption. The script runs deep: marriages should be preserved at all costs, children need two parents under one roof; separation equals failure. The shame hangs in the air whenever someone announces a split, as if they're confessing to a moral failing rather than making a strategic life decision.

But here's where it gets interesting: that script plays out differently depending on where you are in the world. In Latino cultures, machismo, exaggerated masculinity, is prevalent, and infidelity is rampant. In Colombia, 84% of children are born to single mothers. While it is a Catholic country, the expectation that you stay together assumes you were together in the first place. A "normal family" conceptually is the two-parent household, but the numbers tell a very different story.

In gringo culture, there's a different flavor of the same poison: *If you care, you will make it work.* The pressure is more subtle but equally insidious; you should be able to fix it, communicate your way through it, and find the right therapist, technique or intervention. Don't get me wrong, I love therapy, but with the rise of this thinking, we believe any failure is a personal failing (see the different kinds of failure later).

Both scripts miss the same fundamental point: sometimes, the most loving thing you can do is leave.

I've watched friends torture themselves trying to follow these scripts. In the extreme cases, staying in relationships that literally killed them. Their children absorb daily lessons in dysfunction: learning that love looks like fighting, that partnership means enduring misery, that adults don't have agency over their own happiness. Or if they do leave, they apologize for their "broken homes." Here's my radical proposition: What if staying together is no longer the only definition of success, nor always the best outcome? What if a successful partnership is a curious and fun adventure, one that requires two people who genuinely want to be on that adventure together? What if the old script no longer serves anyone, especially the children we claim to be protecting?

Is it easy to be a single parent? No. Is it easier to do it all by myself rather than navigate cross-cultural and irresponsible partners? Yes.

INHERITED WISDOM: MY PARENTS' SUCCESSFUL SEPARATION

I am the child of separation. That fact shaped everything about how I approached my own situation.

Not too unlike my own relationship, my parents weren't married. They separated when I was young and made it work, probably better than if they had stayed together in a loveless relationship. Honestly, I witnessed a healthy breakup. They wrote out an agreement regarding co-parenting and how to handle financial and logistical issues moving forward. They were jointly present and responsible for raising me and treating each other with respect through my college years. I lived with each of them for extended periods. When they lived close, I spent weekends with the other parent. I always thought they broke up well.

That is the reality I grew up with, so I knew it was possible to grow up well with separated parents and have healthy and full relationships with both of them. I had living proof that the cultural script was wrong. I learned a lot living with each of them at different times, both of whom were fully active members of my life. Their romantic status wasn't required for that. My *normal* was parents who weren't together; it has been that way as long as I can remember.

This wasn't abstract theory for me; it was a lived experience. I saw that separation could be done with dignity, that children could thrive, and that sometimes two homes are really better than one dysfunctional household. My parents gave me a different template entirely, one where adult happiness mattered and where children could be loved fiercely from two separate spaces.

When I found myself pregnant and increasingly clear that the relationship wasn't working, I didn't panic about "breaking up a family." I had never seen separation as dysfunction in the first place. What I imagined for my daughter was what I had experienced: two parents who could love her fully without the toxicity of forcing a dead relationship to keep breathing.

It didn't quite work out that way for us, but that's not because the model was wrong. It's because not every person is capable of the emotional maturity required for successful co-parenting. I told a friend, "My parents did a good job of breaking up. I wasn't so good at it." He said, "It takes two people to break up well." That blew my mind. Before that moment, I considered the responsibility entirely mine, but that is not how relationships work; they either work together or they don't. It takes two willing people to make it work. In light of my own experience, I now understand how much my parents poured love into their separation and co-parenting.

THE INTERNATIONAL ADVANTAGE: FREEDOM FROM JUDGMENT

Living abroad gave me something invaluable: distance from the immediate pressure of cultural expectations.

International solo parenting is both easier and harder than doing it in your home culture. Living as a foreigner allowed me some grace to live neither by the local cultural scripts nor the ones of my birth. I got to pick and choose. Easier because the cost of living allows me to be comfortable and seek affordable help. I have built a business that sustains us and feeds my soul. I founded a publishing company that guides people in writing and publishing impactful nonfiction to change the world. The blessing of running a business has not escaped the simple fact that raising my daughter abroad is more challenging because I have had to build a support network in a new place as an adult, away from my extended family and lifelong friends.

However, the freedom from local judgment (and, honestly, American Puritanical expectations) was transformative. I wasn't surrounded by family members asking when we were getting married, or friends who knew his family, or community pressure to make it work. I was in a space where I could make decisions based purely on what was best for my daughter and me, not on what others might think. Part of raising her in Colombia involves recognizing and developing the missing part of her identity that comes from her father. I want Colombia to feel like home for her.

The cultural displacement also let me pick and choose what I wanted to keep from each tradition. From Latino culture, I could take the slow pace of life and the celebration of joy. From gringo culture, I could embrace independence and self-reliance. What I could leave behind was the judgment, the shame, the assumption that my choices were inherently tragic.

Do you have to move abroad in order to leave a toxic relationship? No. I had chosen the expat life years before my daughter ever arrived, so it was a natural extension of my life's decisions. Has it offered many benefits to both of us? Definitely.

This international perspective revealed something crucial: cultural scripts about family are just that, scripts. They're not universal truths. They're stories our particular cultures tell themselves, and you can choose to write a different story.

MY STORY: CHOOSING RELIABLE ABSENCE OVER TOXIC PRESENCE

We met in January. We got together in June, right after I quit my job. I was pregnant before the end of the month, but I didn't know until eight weeks later.

The weekend I got pregnant was the weekend I realized he wasn't who I believed him to be. I could easily say he wasn't who he presented himself to be, but infatuation is a co-creation of willful ignorance. I let myself get swept up by a handsome man, and didn't give myself enough time to see the cracks in the story. After the infatuation faded, there was nothing to build on. It was then clear that perception and reality differed irrevocably. He was not someone I could trust or rely on.

I knew I would be doing this on my own.

Because of how I was raised, I knew we could provide a healthy and fulfilled life without being together. In fact, it was quickly clear that was the only way we could.

I broke up with him when I was eight months pregnant. She was born healthy in a pool in the back of my new yoga studio in a new city, in a foreign country.

The high-level facts are simple: we weren't married. We had only been together a brief time. We didn't have a strong emotional bond. I was pregnant with her at the time of our separation, and she was the result of our union.

She is ten now. He lives in a town four hours away. He has met her five times: when she was 5 days old, 4 months old, 2 years old, 7 years old, and 9 years old. He has not paid a dime in all this time.

For a few years, I was frustrated with him, always wishing he could be reliable and consistent. Then I realized he was; he was *reliably absent* and *consistently manipulative* in our rare communications.

This reframe changed everything for me. I stopped waiting for him to become someone he wasn't. I stopped apologizing to my daughter for his absence. Instead, I began to see his reliable absence as a gift. It meant she wasn't subjected to the emotional whiplash of someone who showed up unpredictably, made promises he couldn't keep, and brought chaos into her stable world. This clarity sparked a surge of energy, enabling me to focus on building and growing my business, taking care of my health, and investing in my daughter's education. Letting go of the story that our life should be something else released me from a huge weight I had been carrying.

I am convinced that reliable absence is infinitely better than toxic presence. It's better than watching adults fight. It's better than a child learning that love means accepting mistreatment and gaslighting. It's better than the exhausting dance of hoping someone will change into who you need them to be.

THE THREE TYPES OF FAILURE (AND WHICH ONE MATTERS)

I've come to understand that there are three kinds of failure:

Failure by Negligence: Not trying, not caring, giving up without effort. This is what people usually think of when they hear "failure": the absence of attempt.

Failure by Design: When systems or relationships are set up in ways that make success impossible. These aren't personal failures; they're structural problems that no amount of individual effort can fix.

Failure by Complexity: When good intentions meet impossible situations, when multiple competing needs can't be met simultaneously, when adult decisions require choosing between imperfect options.

Most people, when they hear about separation, assume it's the first type: that someone didn't try hard enough, didn't care enough, gave up too easily. I have been guilty of this false assumption... of others and of myself.

But my "failure" to stay together was actually *success by design*. I designed a life where my daughter would be protected from toxic dysfunction. I didn't want her to learn disappointment before she learned to walk. I didn't want her to form a sense of self from watching a loveless marriage. I designed a household where she is loved, my needs are met, and we learn and thrive together. I wouldn't permit any man in my life who manipulated and undermined me, even if he were her father. Instead, by design, she has a relationship with her father that prioritizes her well-being over cultural expectations or any notion of how it should be.

The complexity failure...that's the interesting one. Because, truth be told, I couldn't simultaneously give my daughter a father who was present and reliable AND protect us both from the emotional instability he brought. I couldn't simultaneously honor the cultural script of keeping families together AND create the peaceful, secure environment she/we needed to thrive.

When people focus on the "failure" of separation, they're looking at the wrong thing entirely.

SUCCESS REDEFINED: WHAT THRIVING ACTUALLY LOOKS LIKE

My daughter is 10 now. She is growing up without a father; that is true. On the other hand, she has never seen adults scream at each other in her home. She has never had to navigate the emotional minefield of parents who resent each other but stay together "for her sake." She has never been used as a weapon in adult conflicts. She is certainly a priority in my life, but I also want to make sure not to perpetuate the mom-myth that my kids' needs surpass my own. Being single and choosing not to stay in a relationship with someone who made me feel terrible and crazy was, without a doubt, the best decision for me.

My daughter knows she is loved fiercely, completely, without reservation. She knows that the adults in her life make decisions based on what's best for her and them, not based on what others think is right. She's growing up with the radical idea that relationships should add joy to your life, not drain it.

This is what success actually looks like, not the appearance of a *normal* family, but the reality of a healthy one. I have to believe that, growing up with a mom who prioritizes her own mental health and emotional boundaries, models for my daughter that she deserves the same in her life.

What I am grateful for: we have a great life. There remains the possibility that I can find a relationship and a partner who appreciates me for who I am, loves my daughter, and makes it a priority that together, we can grow. This is all I hope for everyone.

The absence of a father's chaos in our daily life isn't a tragedy to be overcome. It's a victory worth celebrating. Every peaceful morning, every bedtime story without adult drama bleeding into her sanctuary, every decision I get to make based purely on her well-being rather than cultural expectations, the dividends of choosing differently.

CLOSING: THE NEW SCRIPT

The larger cultural shift we need isn't just about accepting divorce or separation. It's about fundamentally examining our assumptions about what constitutes family success. I am by no means opposed to marriage or partnership. They can be beautiful things, *but only when there is a connection and mutual commitment.* Staying in a relationship for the sake of the relationship can never be enough.

My daughter is growing up with different models, different possibilities. She's learning that partnership is a choice you make every day, not a trap you fall into. She's learning that love looks like peace, not drama. She's learning that sometimes the most courageous thing adults can do is admit when something isn't working and choose a different approach.

The old script insists that staying together is always better for the children. But children don't need their parents to be together; they need their parents to be healthy. They need adults who take responsibility for their own happiness and who refuse to model dysfunction as love.

So yes—*"Congratulations!"* should sometimes be the response to news of a separation.

Congratulations on choosing your or your child's emotional security over cultural approval. Congratulations on modeling that adults have agency, that they don't have to endure dysfunction, that love doesn't mean suffering.

Congratulations on creating space for something better to grow.

ABOUT THE AUTHOR

Award-winning best-selling author, international speaker & educator, Sierra Melcher is CEO of **Red Thread Publishing**. We are on a mission to support 10,000 people to become successful published authors & thought-leaders. Offering world-class coaching & courses that focus on community, collaboration, and support at every stage of the author process: Write.Publish.Impact.

Sierra has a Master's degree in education and has spoken & taught around the world. Originally from the United States, Sierra lives in Medellín, Colombia, with her daughter.

Sierra Melcher is the author of 18 books to date.

Connect:
redthreadbooks.com
instagram.com/redthreadbooks
linkedin.com/company/red-thread-publishing
Join the community of writers: skool.com/writeyourbook/about

CHAPTER 6

Dichotomy of Divorce and Self-Empowerment

SUMMER JEAN

PREFACE: A GLIMPSE INTO MY OWN SELF-INTROSPECTION OF JOURNALING.

Divorce is a symbolic *"death while still living"* transition. The mystery that has plagued me with divorce is this... the *one* that I loved, who once gave me a sense of place in the world, a deeper meaning to life, a connection so deeply intimate no one else could understand it, the one that made me feel special, desired, important, confident in myself, secure in this world is now the one who can spiral me out of control in seconds flat. Where I am left questioning everything about me, my self-esteem plummets, and my heart aches in a pain that takes my breath away. Even left making me want to cease living at times. The one who once brought me so much safety, solace and love is now the one who has thrown me away, set me aside, and led me astray.

This chapter—and book—is written with the intention of changing the lens through which we see any *split*. The ending of any relationship is complicated, complex, and never a "one-size-fits-all" experience. Growing up, the word *divorce* felt like any other four-letter word you weren't supposed to say as a child—the kind of language that earned you punishment.

Divorce carries a symbolic weight, conjuring images and feelings of failure, dysfunction, broken homes, and the inevitable shadow elephant: everyone outside the relationship quietly wondering who did what. Most of all, the D-word is intimately tied to *shame*. (Perhaps shame is a cousin to divorce, or maybe even a former lover!)

It's time we change the stigma surrounding divorce. It's time we separate the shame from the already painful reality of ending a relationship. We can begin to view divorce as an initiation—a graduation—an induction into a new chapter of life. If we allow it, divorce can become an alchemical process of our own metaphorical death to rebirth. A process so powerful it transforms us in the best way imaginable.

So imagine this: instead of hearing, *"I'm sorry you're going through a divorce,"* from those around you, the people who truly understand the transformational power of pain, loss and grief would say, *"I'm excited for you to go through your divorce—you've got this!"*

THE INTIMACY OF SPLITS, MY PERSONAL JOURNEY

I am an expert in DIVORCE—in more ways than one. Personally and professionally, I have lived nearly every facet of what that word carries. My own childhood was shaped by divorce and all that comes with it: step-parents, step- and half-siblings, moving houses, rotating schedules, new schools, new friends, the constant shift from an old life to a new one. I can honestly say that, growing up, I couldn't wait to leave my family. After my parents divorced, I never truly felt like I belonged.

My dad remarried a woman with two children, and together they had my half-brother. My mom remarried a man who was not a good fit and divorced him five years later, before finally finding stability in her third marriage—a partnership that lasted until her death.

Decades later, time has given me space to heal, grow, and even become grateful for those family dynamics. The friction, conflict, and emotional turmoil eventually transformed into a deeper love within our blended family. I've learned we are not victims of our childhood—we are role players surviving what we cannot control, until we're conscious enough to choose our own path. Still, until that awareness comes, the apple rarely falls far from the tree.

Divorce entered my life again with my first husband—this time as a stay-at-home mother of three young children and a dog. I had just finished my master's degree in counseling, had no income, and was about to begin a full-time, unpaid internship after four years at home. This divorce was my choice. The marriage had become a slow death, stretched across years of children, a house, and our attempt at the American Dream: fall in love, get married, have kids, buy a home, get a dog, and live happily ever after. At 19, wasn't that what everyone was doing? I didn't know any better.

Looking back, I see my truth: I gave everything I could to keep the marriage intact for my children, not wanting to break up their home. But there was no stopping the ending of our vows. In the beginning, we were kids chasing a whimsical kind of love—at least I was. As I grew into myself while playing the roles of wife and mother, I began to wonder who I was outside of them. My husband supported me throughout my undergraduate and graduate degrees, and that became my lifeline. Education was something no one could take away, a foundation I could depend on. It allowed me to stay in the question: *Who am I?* When our split became final, I at least had a path to provide for my children, though our home was now dependent on me alone.

By the time I entered my second long-term relationship—married by common law—I believed divorce was behind me for good. I was wrong. This ending felt written in the stars, unapologetically fated. My soul, it seemed, needed to endure a new species of pain. This divorce blindsided me. It struck harder and deeper than my first, leaving wounds I can still feel years later. It was as if I had been hit by a truck, over and over, left bleeding by the roadside, only to realize the driver was my husband.

This one nearly destroyed me. The active dark nights of the soul were endless, and the passive ones still linger almost three years later. It's hard to explain what this dissolution meant beyond the ego and into the heart. My entire identity had been entwined with my love for my husband, our home, and our life together. When it shattered, I shattered. I had lost myself inside the false sanctity of a "forever" partnership I thought would last until death do us part.

Through my first marriage, I learned that 'love was not enough,' and now, through my second, I have learned that 'some things have nothing to do with love,' but are incredible insights for foreshadowing inner transformation, healing, and self-empowerment.

Professionally, I am an Integrative Sound Psychotherapist and Marriage and Family Therapist specializing in trauma, family systems, relationships, grief, major life transitions, and self-empowerment. I guide individuals from disempowerment to empowerment—helping them transform pain, wounds, and suffering into sources of strength and rebirth. My work spans across the lifespan, from toddlers to elders.

At the core of my practice, I help people learn the language of the soul, so that when life initiations arise, they are not victims of circumstance but victorious creators of their own path. Over the years, I have worked with children of divorce, parents navigating separation, newlyweds, post-divorce co-parents, and even grandparents raising grandchildren because of divorce. If it touches the human experience of love, loss, and transformation—I've walked through it with someone.

SELF-EMPOWERMENT IS A CHOICE, AND IT TAKES ACTION

In both my office and my home, I live a blessed life as a mother of four. Each child has given my life profound meaning—bringing joy, laughter, pain, and sorrow in equal measure. The love I hold for them is beyond words, as is the gratitude I feel for the gift of being their mother.

That love and gratitude are a direct by-product of my relationships with their fathers and the marriages we once shared. For that reason, I could never wish my past to be different. My thoughts are simply, *"if one part of the past was different, what would that mean for my kids, the mother I am today, and our lives together now?"* Each point in the marriage had to play out exactly the way it did for my children to be exactly who they are and for me to be exactly who I am today... and so, I accept, beyond a shadow of a doubt, that divorce is not our enemy, nor is our ex-husband/wife. Divorce is our **initiation into self-transformation**, but *we have to choose* to step into the self-transformation by going through the process with an intention of healing, learning, examining, self-awareness and introspection.

Our partners had to play a specific role that *we* (the divorced) cast them into. The role we unconsciously cast them into served an important and unique purpose for that period of time. What I refer to as "role" is what we "attract" based on Spiritual Laws such as: Law of Karma, Law of Attraction, Law of Balance, etc. The roles we cast others in are straight from within... something in us that magnetically attracted them to us, and us to them. But when that role is no longer healthy, needed, or aligned... it expires. Just as we have to get rid of rotten food after its expiration date, there comes a time when we have to rid ourselves of roles and relationships that no longer serve who we are meant to become. This is how the Universe leads us to an opportunity to grow, expand, evolve and if needed, transform.

Some couples find a way to grow together, transforming as individuals while also evolving the bond between them. But many do not. Every long-term relationship holds countless struggle points—little deaths and rebirths that call both partners inward to do the work of love, for *self* and *other*.

Those who endure learn to dance with the shifting power dynamics, accepting and adapting as each rises into new levels of growth and emotional maturity. Those who part ways often hit a disconnect so deep it unravels the very fabric of repair. Chaos replaces connection, and survival takes precedence over union with the one who may have hurt, betrayed, or abandoned them. When that point is reached, the relationship itself cries out for nothing less than a total reset.

There is a GRIT to long-term relationships that not everyone has. But if we begin to change the *perception* of any "SPLIT," I believe we can nourish and grow the grit needed for healthy partnerships when the second, third or fourth chance comes around, because another relationship *always* comes around. As humans, our WELL-being requires a sense of belonging, connection and a profound knowing that we matter. Without these qualities, we simply do not thrive.

Discomfort, by its very nature, triggers an instinct to seek relief. This is why many people never truly heal, learn, or grow after divorce. Instead of taking accountability, accepting responsibility, and learning how to do things differently—or better—in the future, they focus on blaming and shaming the other person while chasing their own comfort.

Yet it is through pain that we grow, expand, and discover what needs to change. It is through suffering that we are called inward—into the darkness of our own shadows. Facing our fears and stepping into the unknown future is terrifying. We don't know what we'll uncover: old memories, unhealed traumas, buried wounds. We don't know which shortcomings, false beliefs, or distorted perceptions will be exposed—or what we'll be required to own and improve upon.

Many avoid this work entirely. They blame and shame others, clinging to their stories and emotions, seeking validation for why they were "right" or "justified" in their role as husband, wife, or partner. For some, the weight of what lies within feels unbearable. So they drink, chase pleasure, rush into new relationships, or distract themselves in any way possible—avoiding the very opportunity that pain is offering them.

Any SPLIT, whether in marriage, family, or in our self-identity, *is* this opportunity. A chance to go inward and ask the deeper, more honest questions that can only be answered from the sweet, small voice within. This marks the beginning of the transformation process from powerless to empowered. Self-examination through pain, suffering, grief, loss and survival begins to turn into the GRIT discussed previously in regard to long-term relationships! Except this grit is to keep living day after day, week after week, towards self-empowerment, all the while looking within for how to live life differently because the pain of the split is not something we ever want to experience again. So we turn inward and introspect, paying attention to one's own mind, body and soul.

What does it mean to "go inward?" Our culture rarely teaches this, yet with rising stress, mental health struggles, divorce, and even suicide, a shift in consciousness is underway. Instead of relying only on experts to diagnose and fix us, we're learning to approach well-being holistically —honoring the mind-body connection and our spiritual nature. Inner work becomes the practice of self-awareness through tools like yoga, meditation, journaling, therapy, and other healing practices.

This shift is especially liberating for women. Not long ago, many could not survive comfortably without a man to provide, particularly mothers raising children. We are the descendants of a generation shaped by the Great Depression and wartime, where survival left deep imprints of shame around "failed" marriages and "broken" families. While today's youth may see divorce as normal, many parents still carry hidden guilt and shame, along with the stress of raising children across two households.

Shame must be named and felt as part of the grief process. The grief of divorce is not the same as death—some say it is harder, because the person remains in your life through conversations, co-parenting, or shared memories. It wounds not only through loss, but also through inflicting blows to self-worth, esteem and identity. We often don't realize how much of our value we've tied to partners, family, or roles—until those bonds are broken and out in the public's eye to view and discuss.

Taking our power back requires going inward with radical self-honesty. It means asking vulnerable questions in the quiet space of the heart and soul, and inviting the ego to step aside. The ego—rooted in fear, attachment, and control—is often what fueled the pain *and* the split in the first place. True healing asks us to seek guidance from a deeper place within. And while we all have the ability to travel inward, the journey can feel tender and overwhelming. Because of the tenderness, the intense emotions and ways we protect ourselves, we may not easily access these depths by ourselves; we need a trusted guide—a therapist, mentor, spiritual teacher, or friend—to walk alongside us.

A GUIDE TO GOING INWARD

Here are a few reflective questions to sit with before answering. Give each one space to breathe, allowing the response to emerge through body sensations, feelings, emotions, memories, images, or visions. Let your pen simply record the experience of introspection, bringing what lives inside you into the physical world. This practice creates healthy separation—shifting from personal attachment to gentle observation. From this place, you can examine through the heart and soul without judgment, expectation, or old beliefs.

Before moving into the list of inquiries, set the tone for self-exploration. Find a quiet, undisturbed space and soothe your nervous system with grounding rituals: light a candle, dim the lights, wrap yourself in a blanket, brew your favorite tea, or play soft instrumental music. Think of it as a sacred date with yourself—make it intentional, romantic, and special. Protect this space, and don't take it for granted.

Remember, this journey is about exploring the dynamics of love. How we show up for self-love is just as vital as how we give love. Begin with intention, begin with love.

IDENTITY & SECURITY

- What is my identity?
- Where is my sense of security in this world?
- What role have my relationships played for my sense of security, identity and self-value/worth?
- What do I put my faith and trust in?
- What are my inner core beliefs, values, and virtues?

SELF-LOVE & EXPRESSION

- How do I desire to be loved?
- How do I show up for myself—honoring my soul, personality, and unique treasures? How do I love myself?
- How do I speak intimately with myself? Do I even like myself?
- How do I allow my self-expression to be heard and seen?
- Do I allow others to truly see me?
- Where is my self-esteem and confidence?
- What gives me value and worth?

EMOTIONS, FEAR & HEALING

- Where does fear live in the depths of my mind?
- How do I overcome the paradigms of past trauma and wounds?

- How do I fight for power? Do I even need to fight?
- What makes me angry—truly angry? How far back does my anger go?
- How do I express anger, resentment, or rage? Do I project it outward, or turn it inward?
- Where do I still sabotage my own growth, potential, and connection with my higher self, the universe, and God?

SPIRIT & PURPOSE

- What are my Spiritual beliefs?
- What passions, talents, and gifts do I bring to life?
- How do I connect with Nature and the Universal Wisdom of Nature?
- What prayers, mantras, and affirmations help guide me?
- What lights me up? What brings me joy?

VISION & CREATION

- If there were no obstacles, and anything were possible, what life would I create? What relationships would I have?
- How would this dream life *look?* How would it *feel?*
- Do I have more than one dream life? If so, what are they? Write them all out—with no blocks, no limitations.

CAN WE CELEBRATE YET?

I hope by now, we have come full circle to the true DICHOTOMY OF DIVORCE AND SELF-EMPOWERMENT. Recognizing the potency of pain, heartache, loss, desperation and yes, SHAME. Divorce can feel like the ultimate breaking, but really, it can be the ultimate *making*. Consciously and intentionally giving less attention to the ending of a relationship, and more attention to the birth of a *new Self*. Where we get to drastically stop, examine, and reassess how we are showing up in life, how we are making decisions, and if we are authentically living as our

True Self. No longer victims of circumstance, powerless, and unconsciously playing out roles. That's pretty exciting!! When we seize the opportunity to reclaim who we are and who we want to become, that is worth celebrating! Are you grateful for your SPLIT yet?

ABOUT THE AUTHOR

Summer Jean, owner of Agami Karma Therapy, is a seasoned Integrative Sound Psychotherapist and mother of four, dedicated to empowering others to heal. Combining Western Psychology and Eastern Philosophy, she helps clients overcome trauma, fears, and major life transitions with a deeper sense of Self. With over 20 years of experience and a distinguished speaking career in the medical, educational, and mental health fields, Summer's work focuses on overcoming obstacles and promoting mind-body-soul balance. Passionate about Spirituality and the human experience, she inspires others to create purposeful, empowered lives.

Connect:
   Website www.agamikarmatherapy.com
   Blog www.agamikarmatherapy.com/blog
   on all platforms: @summerjean4om

CHAPTER 7

How Far?

DR. KATHERINE HUMPHREYS

They were the longest two miles of my life. He was running after the car, banging on the trunk, distraught and yelling for me to stop. I was gripping the steering wheel white-knuckled, crying and shaking. It was not my intention for this to be so dramatic. I didn't want to inflict the pain of being left, I just didn't know how to slip away quietly. I wanted to do something constructive, less hopeless—I wanted to put some distance between us and our situation.

My mom had flown in to help me navigate the split. Her love was best expressed by helping in a time of need, and her being there meant everything. I insisted on driving, knowing I couldn't sit idly as a passenger. I yearned for something to distract myself. I had to be the one on the gas pedal so I wouldn't be tempted to turn the car around for more discussion and another chance. Was I running because this is what I resorted to when things felt too much, or was this a necessary escape to find a solution and, ultimately, myself?

It took six hours and half the width of Texas before the gas tank, and my tears started to dry. At that point, I was still shaking, still questioning every mile, still not sure I could go through with leaving. I was learning that I was not "good" at breaking up. My fear of disappointing others, of being a disappointment, was intense. I did not have a plan for deviating from the script I was raised with—the one society set forth as an ideal: Meet someone, get married, and stay married at all costs. There was no divorce in my family. Pushing forward, trying harder, and making it work was the only option. Yet, my marriage was in clear distress, and nothing had been able to resuscitate it. It was failing, I was failing. So, what now?

HOW IT BEGAN

Three years earlier, I had moved across the country. Having chosen a job and a place that was a great fit for me. I was feeling confident in my choices. I was focused on growing programs and getting to know my new community. I wasn't thinking about marriage, but what was meant to be a casual fling turned into far more.

We went from that first night to many in a row. I remember giving him a casual line about how I was "dating around;" the response was something to the effect of "them or me." If I wanted to continue seeing "new guy," no other dates. Fine, I thought, I am comfortable with monogamy, and who was I to ignore this kind of interest?

What started in August led to an engagement in October. We had some of the obligatory discussions about family, values, about the future. Looking back, I can't say I would have had the wherewithal to know what I was looking for in a husband. Now, I know I was looking for a partner, an equal, someone who wouldn't leave me if there was conflict. The truth was that neither of us knew what we wanted, too young to truly know ourselves as individuals. Still, we forged ahead. He proposed with a grand, romantic gesture that I felt I couldn't say "no" to. What was the worst that could come of it? We were established in life, surely we were in a good position to be married.

SIGNS

We had fun in the time between our engagement and marriage; I didn't recognize any signs that would deter me from moving from a Miss to a Mrs. In reality, I was naive and didn't know what to look for. We hadn't given ourselves the time to face and overcome challenges, time to test our compatibility.

Quickly after marriage, there was pressure to move. I left a job and the city that had suited me. We bought a home. It all felt very grown-up, only neither of us had the fully developed brains of an adult. We were limping by on low amounts of emotional intelligence. We didn't have a clue how to disagree or fight in a constructive way. I was good at antagonizing, and he was not good at managing his anger. One night, we had a fight and I ran down into the kitchen. I was caught backed into a corner, and he let a fist fly, denying it almost immediately. I wanted to believe it didn't happen. I wasn't that good at ignoring things, though.

That night set into motion our demise.

Within a year, we had moved again. I was willing to put my career aside, holding tightly to that marital script. It was around this time that the topic of kids was coming up. He said I could have them and could stay home with them. Wasn't that what I should want?

Our new home in the country was peaceful, but isolated. It added to the pressure of a marriage under siege. I would weaponize my words, and he would respond in anger. I became adept at dodging household items. We sought help, but it was not enough. Despite having none of the "typical" problems, infidelity, financial stress, addiction, our relationship was spiraling out of control. During one fight, he left for three days. On another occasion, he drove up a freeway off-ramp and spun around at the last moment. To combat the chaos, I ran longer and longer distances to work through our issues in my mind. But I couldn't log enough miles to resolve the situation.

I started to share with some close friends. The more I shared, the more I realized this was something I would encourage anyone I cared for to get out of. Yet, I constantly reminded myself of "until death do us part." But what if we just took a little break? What if we pressed "pause?" For a people-pleaser, the ultimate rejection of asking someone for a divorce was a big leap. I didn't feel I had the right to reject someone in that way. Besides, what would people think? But what if a separation healed the wounds in our relationship? It was worth a try.

When a job offer came, I approached it with him as a very temporary sort of thing. I would leave the state to take this great opportunity, a step forward in my career, and in the meantime, it would give us both the time and space to determine the way forward. It would be a pause. I called our moms and made a plan to go.

Looking back, I was simply too afraid to deal the harsh blow. He probably realized that, so he was determined to chase down the car. Deep down, I knew the pain we inflicted on each other was ultimately about our mutual fear of rejection; instead of being vulnerable, we built walls and relied on manipulation, stubbornness, and selfishness, all to avoid our own suffering. We wanted the marriage to work. I had loved him, and I believed he had loved me, but things had gone too far. To stay, I would have had to lose all respect for myself; and after trying marriage and failing, I didn't have much to spare. We had clearly both lost respect for each other. We were hanging on by a thread. And so I left. I ran. But I couldn't outrun the guilt; it was as heavy as a weighted blanket.

Nobody was meant to be a winner in our tug-of-war. We didn't recover; we weren't meant to recover. Two years later, a colleague sheepishly handed me a stack of papers from the fax machine: it was a divorce notice. I was lucky to have an education and close friends and family for support; I know not everyone has this. I also know that anyone in an unhealthy situation should still try to do what it takes to change it.

COURAGE

Courage is the ability to do something that frightens one. I had been operating from a place of fear and had avoided hard decisions from the get-go. I know now that I was so uncomfortable facing the emotions that would come from listening to my intuition that I later forced my ex to make the decision for us. I was afraid of his, and everyone's, reactions; afraid of being a disappointment.

I now had to summon the courage to dig in and learn about myself. I had to face the "why" behind my own behaviors. I read, I studied, I sought counseling. I came away with a better understanding of my own patterns and vulnerabilities. Armed with this insight, I realized I had to be more intentional about my relationships, factoring in my communication style, love languages, and triggers.

It took some time before I felt ready to dip my toe back into the dating pool. Part of me felt like, "Who was I to get another chance?" I had made a mess of it when others stuck together and followed the script. But I have since accepted that there is no gold star for staying in a relationship that is toxic to one or both partners.

Initially, I didn't get it right. After my divorce, I swung for the fences and met someone who was the opposite of my ex. He was a man with a tender heart who let me take the lead. But like most of us, he had his own issues that manifested into a gambling addiction exacerbated by underlying mental illness. Once again, resentment reared its ugly head, and I felt as much reproach for myself as I did for him. I have a strong and angry inner critic that I am constantly working to tame. The relationship ended in a painful and dramatic way, inciting new trauma. We had lived together as common-law partners, and I had known for a year or more that the relationship needed to end. This was clear evidence that I still struggled to end unions constructively; I still let things drag on. I had to reconnect with my inner self, gather my strength, and start over again.

After this, I had more clarity. I spent less time wallowing in guilt and shame and began to see my core nature as a compass. Maybe I didn't have to completely change who I was to be with someone; maybe I needed a partner who could complement the parts of me that will likely never change. And maybe I could accomplish this without either of us having to give up anything of ourselves

INTENTIONALITY & HEALING

I devoured the book, 'The Secret,' and took away the need to be intentional about my next partner. I wasn't in a hurry, but I felt I could trust myself not to make the same mistakes. For the first time, I was a fully-grown adult living on my own, a woman with a list of ideal traits for a partner taped to her headboard. I was determined not to settle until I fulfilled that list.

I knew I needed to be ready just in case, so I was deliberate with myself. I made sure I felt secure in my singleness by exercising, joining clubs, and focusing on my career. I relied on my old adage of saying "yes" to opportunities–but I made sure my efforts served me in a healthy way.

I didn't believe in love at first sight, but at a speed-dating event, I felt a flash of soul recognition when I saw him walk into the room. We only had six minutes to talk, but the next morning I had an email message that read, "Six minutes was not long enough, can I see you again?"

We took it slow. This guy met so many of my criteria– well-traveled, open-minded, humble yet confident. He was comfortable with who he was as a person, a quiet confidence that I am still learning from. He was divorced, as well. We didn't need to speak poorly of our exes. This was a good sign. We didn't have to agree on things, but could listen to each other's points of view. We had different backgrounds, and we were headed to similar places. We wanted to be time-rich and see the world. Our personalities were quite different but compatible. We laughed. He could really make me laugh (and still does)!

Fast forward. At the time of writing this, we have been together for over seventeen years. We have children, one of the strongest tests of a relationship. We have faced trials and tribulations, but we have gotten through those by ultimately respecting each other. I am quick to compliment; people need to hear that you love and support them. It is important to build your partner up, not break them down. He, in turn, really listens. He lets me vent without taking it personally, without needing to offer a solution. He shows his love by seeking to resolve situations without anger or blame. We have learned how to fight; it's okay to disagree and go to bed upset, as long as we wake up the next day and keep trying to move forward together. With his support, I earned my Ph.D., obtained promotions, started a business, co-wrote a book, and began consulting, all while we grew the company he started. We've acted on our shared passion for investing in real estate and built a portfolio. We've designed a life that works for us.

FAR ENOUGH

"Far enough" is where bad days become good days. Far enough is where problems become solutions. I no longer run long distances. I don't feel the need to. I can work things out over a shorter distance. I don't worry that my partner is going to leave me, or that I need to leave him. We show up for each other. I also know that physical or psychological abuse has no place in a relationship, that too often we excuse away abusive behavior and abandon our own security. We have a right to ensure we are safe in our own homes. I want to teach my children that they do not need to self-abandon to find a healthy relationship.

I don't believe there is a certain age for marriage or a certain amount of time a couple should date. Personally, I was too young. I believe there needs to be an understanding of oneself, such that you can navigate relationship trials constructively. I try harder now to pause before reacting. I try to consider what I say and how I say it. I am highly challenged by parenting. I don't always get it right. Patience is not a virtue of mine, and that is my reality. I am learning to allow myself to mess up. To give grace to myself and to my partner. I no longer worry that disagreements are going to spiral out of control.

FORGIVENESS & MOVING FORWARD

I felt guilty and broken for a time; I did not want to align myself with the term "divorce." I still have to fight the shame that burns when I think about all the time and effort my family and friends put into my wedding. The word "split" was not supposed to be in my vocabulary, let alone a chapter of my story. But I've come to acknowledge that my first marriage was a place in my journey, a journey I do not regret. I still exchange kind words with my first in-laws. I feel them rooting for me, and I am rooting for them and my ex. I want to extend forgiveness for the young woman I was and the young man my ex-husband was. I see a bright future. I recently read a quote: "If I forgive me, I can forgive him. And so it is all forgiven. We are all free to go."

ABOUT THE AUTHOR

Dr. Katherine Humphreys is currently living in Medellin, Colombia, with her British husband, two children, and their recently adopted English Bull Terrier. Although Las Vegas remains their home base, the family previously lived in a small coastal village in the Dominican Republic. Drawing on their adventures in over 40 countries, Katherine is writing a graphic novel adventure series for young readers.

Prior to her current life as a **worldschool Mom**, Dr. Humphreys was a university administrator. She spent decades managing teams, consulting, presenting at conferences, and serving in professional association roles. She still wears several hats, including managing a real estate portfolio and helping to run the family business. She also serves as a chief logistical officer for all the family's travel and as an 'author mentor' for a publishing company. She seeks joy in exercise, new experiences, and quality time with the people she loves.

Connect:
www.linkedin.com/in/dr-katherine-humphreys-302453376
www.facebook.com/katie.s.humphreys
www.instragram.com/katherinehumphreys

CHAPTER 8

Listening for Grace

DR. ERICA ANNE LOVE

Listen to your life.
See it for the fathomless mystery it is...
All moments are key moments,
And life itself is grace.

— FREDERICK BUECHNER (1991)

I have always cherished silence and solitude. Even as a child, I needed my own time—my heart took flight in the quiet of fresh snow in a forest, the evening call of the loon on the lake, or the morning stillness of the water broken only by the slap of a jumping fish. I spent hours curled up quietly with my books and journals, writing poems, songs, and letters to the world; a vividly silent dialogue in my head with a voice I rarely revealed to others.

Silence wasn't emptiness to me; it was possibility.

When I was in sixth grade, I remember a field trip to cabins deep in the woods. One night, our teachers led us down a narrow trail and, one by one, left each of us to sit alone among the trees for an hour. The night was cool, earthy, damp, and dark. My classmates later confessed they were afraid—the rustle of unseen animals, the creak of branches in the wind, unnerving them.

But I wasn't afraid. In that hush, and in the solitude that held it, I felt something loosen inside me. With no one to perform for and nothing to prove, my mind drifted past the edge of the trail and into its own wild landscape. I could follow thoughts without interruption, hear the faint whispers of an inner voice I hadn't yet learned to name. It was more than quiet—it was freedom. Just me, the breathing forest, and the unbroken company of myself.

That early love of stillness became my anchor. I didn't yet know that one day I would need it for survival.

THE BODY I LIVE IN

At seventeen, a rare cerebral vascular spinal condition landed me in a wheelchair for months. Doctors weren't sure if I would live, and if I did, whether I'd be able to walk again. It was my first reckoning with the body I live in—not the one I'd imagined, but the one that would accompany me for the rest of my life.

While I felt grateful to be alive, I'll also admit I felt betrayed by my body. I remember crying at 17, asking my mom, "What boy will find someone in a wheelchair attractive?" Now, some thirty years later, the question still echoes in different forms. Who wants a partner who can't walk with them?

I don't think anyone intentionally discriminates against people like me, someone with a physical disability. I mean, you'd have to be a real jerk, right? However, the reality is that a good majority of people, up to a certain age, are able-bodied-centric in their ideas of what constitutes an "attractive partner," a "capable leader," or a "brilliant thinker."

At age 24, my vascular condition caused another medical crisis, leaving me with permanent spinal damage. I was body-shamed by my first husband, who was insensitive to the grief I was grappling with. This experience fueled a stubborn determination not to be defined by my condition and disability.

In the years that followed my first divorce, I became an expert at pushing through. I finished college, started a career, moved cross-country knowing absolutely no one there, and bought a home. I traveled for work, said yes to challenges, ascended the career ladder, and became the kind of person people described as "driven" and "resilient," a "natural leader." Solitude was not loneliness—it was the place I restored my reserves so I could show up in these ways. Silence provided the place where I could feel whole again.

AND THEN CAME LOVE

I lived as a single woman for almost fifteen years after my first marriage ended. I wasn't really looking for someone to complete me. In fact, I reveled in having complete control over my home environment. Every room of my house was decorated to reflect me, arranged to suit how I wanted to live. After spending time with married friends, I often thought, "Thank goodness I don't have to compromise my life in that way." The truth was, I couldn't picture myself marrying again, or even living with anyone. Ever. My solitude had become its own kind of sanctuary.

When I considered the logistics of inviting someone into my life, I often confessed to friends that I wasn't sure I'd ever be willing to compromise on sharing my space. I used to joke that dating apps had it all wrong—they shouldn't just ask how close you wanted to live to a potential match, but how far away they should live to guarantee no surprise pop-ins.

But when I hit my mid-forties, having completed my doctorate degree and being selected as a dean at a local college, I was finally ready to explore whether a partner could walk beside me without crowding out what I needed to thrive. And so, I decided to dive into the dating pool.

Being a very busy professional and a covert introvert, I turned to online dating. At the time, there was still a stigma associated with using online dating to find a long-term, meaningful relationship; I was a little embarrassed to admit to any colleagues that I was using this method to connect with someone who might enrich my life. But I didn't really see any other option for meeting potential partners in my mid-40s that was as efficient as online dating.

I discovered I hated dating. It's not that I don't know how to make conversation. If you want to debate the meaning of life, whether humanity has a shot in hell of not destroying itself in the next century, or how to show up as a leader, then I am your date! But please, put me out of my misery when dating becomes a meaningless, energy-sucking performance or an exercise in superficial, inauthentic, judgmental conversations.

I admit that what I probably hated most about dating was the vulnerability of showing up to a first date. I had to mentally brace myself for the moment when the person I had only met virtually saw that I had a physical disability. It wasn't something that one could tell from any of my posted pictures because at the time, I wasn't "enough" in my own mind, so I chose not to include it in my profile.

And then I met Alf.

Alf made me feel seen. He fell in love with me, not despite my physical challenges but, he said, because they shaped who I was. We married within three years of meeting, and my carefully curated home became a shared space with him and his two children. I redecorated rooms for the kids, kept my own bathroom and closet sacred, and thought I had successfully struck a balance between togetherness and space.

There was much joy: waking up next to someone, sharing reflections on the day, debating ideas, exploring new places, hearing laughter drift down the hall, and being pulled into activities I wouldn't have tried alone.

THE SLOW WEARING DOWN

At the same time, my pain, though never extreme by the numbers, was constant—an unwelcome hum beneath every moment. This, along with mobility limitations that were gradually getting worse, took more and more energy. Even so, I told myself to "cowboy up" and push through.

For me, living with chronic pain is like having a shadow I can't step out of. It's there when I wake, follows me into every conversation, every plan, every attempt at rest. Most days, I've learned to work around it, to smile through it, and to carry it so well that other people forget it's there.

I rarely forget.

It has sometimes been an isolating experience. You can try to describe it, but words slip short of the truth. You can measure it on a scale, but the numbers flatten it. And so, I carried it mostly alone. And the isolation wasn't just from the pain itself—it was from how quietly it rewrote my life. Activities I once loved slipped off the calendar. Invitations became calculations. I started guarding my energy the way some people guard their savings, measuring out how much I could spend in a day.

While the pain that consumed my energy and attention was physical, I've also come to see it as a reflection of a deeply buried emotional pain I did not give myself space to hear—grief that would not fade and anxiety that kept my muscles coiled tight. My nervous system began to fray.

In early 2020, my body dealt another blow: a brain hemorrhage. I spent over a month in the ICU. I have little memory of that time, but I do know that my family didn't know if I would live or die. I came home just before the pandemic shut everything down, suddenly wheelchair-bound in a house constantly full of people as we "sheltered in place."

Many months later, as we emerged from the pandemic and the aftermath of my health crisis, our lives were permanently changed, and moments of solitude became almost non-existent. Alf and I worked remotely, and the kids were only out of the house when attending school. We were together all the time.

Ironically, even as I longed for quiet and solitude, I filled every quiet moment with mental distraction: work, social media, books, and television. I realize now I was afraid of my body, I felt betrayed by my body, and I was angry with my body. I was also burying anger I felt towards my husband and kids—simply because they were able-bodied. They had the choice to walk, run, bike, leap, dance, and more. And...like most able-bodied people...largely took it for granted.

I no longer knew how to enjoy the quiet stillness, avoiding a truth that was in my bones: this life was unsustainable.

THE BREAK

Then, one August evening in 2024, my body said, "Enough."

Following a massage that was meant to ease my legs, a wave of unbelievable pain shot from my back through my hip and down my leg. I curled up and began to cry. Alf suggested the hospital, but the thought of going back into that system—after all my medical trauma—was unbearable.

In the days that followed, something shifted. The doctors later called it a psychotic break. I can only describe it as being caught in a bright, unstoppable current. Images, ideas, and connections poured through me—patterns about the world, the nature of humanity, the way everything is connected. Time dissolved. I had no sense of hours or days, and I didn't want to return to what had been my reality.

In the middle of that current, I remember a moment of absolute clarity. It felt less like thinking and more like being shown something ancient and true: that my body holds knowledge to heal itself; knowledge that can be tapped when I listen closely in the stillness. And with that realization, a wondrous space was opened in my brain.

For the first time in years, every muscle unclenched itself. All the tension I had been carrying — the pain, the striving, the grief — melted away. I felt light and expansive, as if I were dissolving into something infinite.

THE DISTORTION

But, my mind—under extreme strain— also spun darker stories. I became convinced Alf had harmed me. I cried silently while lying in bed next to him, plotting an escape and mentally saying goodbye. I then faked unconsciousness so that he'd take me to the hospital, where I told my delusional story to the staff, and was eventually placed in a psych ward. One foot in reality, one in another world.

Those hallucinations were not real, and yet in some way, the core message they carried was a truth my body had been trying to tell me: you must leave to live. Not because Alf was actively harming me, but because my body was screaming at me that the way I was living was unsustainable. I could no longer ignore it.

LISTENING

When I left the hospital, I couldn't be near Alf without my body tensing, my pain spiking. This wasn't about his worth as a man—it was about my body's truth. My nervous system, already threadbare, was screaming for stillness and silence in order to mend.

With the help of a friend and therapist, I realized I needed space to heal. Months later, I knew that the transformation I had undergone meant ending our marriage. It was one of the hardest truths I've ever spoken. Women are more often inclined to serve everyone else first, to hold the family together no matter the cost to ourselves. But there is nothing noble about self-erasure. Real courage is claiming the space you need to nourish your soul.

GRACE

The Stoics wrote that we cannot control what happens to us, only how we respond. Stoic author Ryan Holiday calls stillness "the key" because it allows us to choose a response with clarity instead of reactivity. The reclaiming of space and stillness in my life didn't erase the pain, but it gave me a place to meet it without panic or denial. It reminded me that the noise—the distractions, the pushing through—wasn't strength at all. True strength was being willing to be with myself exactly as I was, without rushing to escape.

In the days and weeks that followed a final decision to end my marriage to Alf, I began to learn how to listen to my body. In doing so, I finally was able to let go of the belief that my body had failed me all this time and instead saw all the ways in which it had been designed to save me. And in the stillness as I listened, I heard inside me a familiar voice—a voice I would later name Grace.

Grace guided me to stop numbing my body with medication. She led me to healthier food, meditation, and the discipline of sitting quietly with myself—even when the quiet was uncomfortable. She made me weep for the suffering of the world and for its beauty. She reminded me that I am more than what I do or endure—that I am held, even without answers.

She also showed me how far modern life has pulled us from the wisdom of our ancestors—those who lived by the cycles of the sun and seasons, who understood the body's need for rest, who listened to the land as much as to each other. We live now in a culture of perpetual noise, our nervous systems lit up like switchboards until we burn out. Grace reminded me that my body, like the earth, requires time to renew.

Holiday writes that stillness is "the doorway to self-mastery, discipline, focus, and clarity." Grace has become my teacher in that same way. She slows me down enough to see what is true, to choose what matters, and to endure what I cannot change without letting it harden me. She reminds me that stillness is not inaction; it is the most intentional action I can take.

I don't pretend to fully understand Grace. She is presence, a quiet companion, a reminder that there is wisdom beyond noise, beyond intellect. She is the reason I now trust that life itself is a kind of symphony—every pain, loss, joy, and meeting part of a perfect, if mysterious, design.

THE COST AND THE GIFT OF THE SPLIT

I grieve for what happened to my husband and me in August. I grieve the loss of our marriage, the love, and the dreams we had, and I honor the chapter Alf and the kids played in my life. I have also grieved for the years I drowned out my own stillness because I was afraid of what it might say, of what I might hear.

I no longer question the necessity of what happened to cause our split. In the end, it was not about leaving him—it was about returning to myself. It was about waking up to my life, to the path of self-destruction I had been on because I was bottling up my grief. It was about reclaiming the solitude I needed.

In the silence and unseen, I sometimes see clearly how every step and every word were all exactly what needed to be. In the countless pauses life pressed into my path, through illness and limitation, each moment was a rehearsal for the life I have now, a life that chooses stillness not out of necessity, but out of reverence.

Dear readers, please hear me: we live in a world in which the chaos and noise of daily life far exceeds the capacity of our psyche and nervous system to absorb it. Our insistence on creating space for stillness and solitude is not a luxury. It is a matter of survival. Carving out silence for your own wholeness is not selfish. It is the only viable response to an existential threat to humanity's existence. The modern world will not hand you stillness—you must claim it. Somewhere in that quiet, your own Grace is waiting to speak.

When she speaks...believe her.

ABOUT THE AUTHOR

Dr. Erica Anne Love is the founder and CEO of BeCourageous Leadership, a consulting practice that supports leaders and institutions navigating the changing landscape of work and human development. Her approach integrates systems strategy with reflective practice, helping others lead with clarity, presence, and purpose. Erica is also the author of the forthcoming children's book *Be* and is currently launching a women-led coffeehouse and coworking community rooted in human connection and abundance. Her chapter, *Listening for Grace*, draws from a year of personal transformation and exploration of practices that foster connection, healing, and the capacity to live and lead from what matters most.

Connect:
  www.becourageousleadership.com
  www.linkedin.com/in/ericaannelove
  www.instagram.com/ericaannelove

CHAPTER 9

I Define Me

ALLISON BANEGAS

Two divorces. That's right, two. I remember the immense weight of the first, how heavy and dreadful it felt, especially with society's views on marriage and children. The judgment echoed from every corner of the world where marriage and motherhood are highly valued. By the time I was thirty-two, I accepted that the world saw me as a failure: three children by two fathers. It felt like a death sentence; I had barely started to live as an adult after all I had learned.

Then the negative thoughts would hit me all at once.

Who is going to want to be around me? I am not good enough to be with.

I failed my kids.
I failed my family.
I failed myself.

I was destroying myself with the thoughts and words society made me believe. Separating from toxic cycles felt like the smallest of my worries. What no one warned me about was all the glass pieces you are left to pick up. The damage it creates not only for yourself, but also for your kids. There is no perfect way through divorce, and I have two as proof. The struggles I faced with my first divorce, at only 17 years old, were brutal. I was still a child myself, learning to be an adult when I had no clue how to even be a child.

Divorce brought out many ugly memories. Thoughts rose from past experiences. Trauma. Triggers. I am a victim of sexual assault and rape since age 4, and that is based on the experiences that I can remember. Divorce meant I was once again going through emotions all alone, but this time with the responsibility of two children. My first divorce made me determined to shield my kids from feeling abandoned as I had. A problem with my first divorce was that my own family loved having him around more than they wanted me around. But that was normal. Going back to when I was about nine years old, a relative had assaulted me several times until he was finally caught. The importance of this was that it changed the narrative. It's a common experience in many Hispanic families for children to be left to fend for themselves while adults look the other way. I struggled as a teenage mom to protect myself from my own thoughts. I used my kids' well-being as my arsenal to keep pushing. I wanted to be and do better for them. I felt that they deserved as much normalcy as I could provide for them.

Divorce is never an easy process; it's not easy being a child of a split. My mother and my biological father were never married. He wasn't a part of my life until I was much older, and the absence carved its own wounds. I remember how broken and unwanted I felt because I didn't have the father figure I needed. I saw all my classmates with their parents, and I envied them. I wanted to be cared for. Protected. I remember how my mother worked long hours as a housekeeper after she had my brother. She poured herself into others because it was what she had been taught to do. My grandmother had left her when she was 15 to care for her younger siblings, and she stayed in that role.

I remember the day I asked my mother why my father left. All I had was one video where he appeared, from when they lived in Los Angeles before I was born. The feelings... the thoughts. Did he not love me? Did I mean anything to him? Was I just not enough for him? The only words my mother could offer were that he was not good enough and that he did not deserve me. It still did not help. The child version of me felt abandoned. Unloved. Worthless. I remember creating online profiles, desperately searching for any trace of where and who my father was.

My father-wound only grew bigger, and it created so many problems in my life. The first assault I can visually remember. I was around 4 years old. The man who collected the rent was at the door asking for my mother and my aunt. Luckily, there was a chain on the door, and it could only open so much. That's when he kneeled and asked me to get closer. Naïve, I obeyed. Thinking that I'd seen him around my mom and aunt, I thought I was ok. Wrong. He touched my private areas. Luckily, my aunt came back. That was the first time. I felt strange, lost, and confused. No one knew that this had happened. I have seen this man again around the town I grew up in. He just stares at me as if he has seen a ghost.

Next was my uncle. New Year's 2000. A night to celebrate. A night to set your New Year's resolutions. I was at a party with friends and family. The party had the typical Spanish music playing, food, and the grown-ups were drinking. I remember the girls that I was playing with. I was 9 and we were just playing around. We decided to play hide-and-seek in a bedroom. I tried to contain my giggles while hiding. What could go wrong? My uncle walked into the room, and at first, I thought he was in on the game. The girls and I were hiding in the closet area, thinking, "We are playing." It was normal. They pushed me to the front. The other girls were curled up behind me... but they had this terrified look on their faces. And then, it happened. My uncle found me and started to touch me. I was distraught. I was confused. The innocence of childhood was stolen from me at that moment.

After this, I had a conversation with the girls and learned that this had been happening to them for a while. That was the last time I saw them until I went to high school. They had spoken out about him and been classified as liars. My mom kept me away from them, thinking it was best not to engage in those problems. But what my mom didn't know was that it had happened to me several times. The last time it happened, my younger brother witnessed and spoke about it. And that's when it all started. I was the black sheep of the family. Everyone told me to "tell the truth," but when I did, I was accused of tearing the family apart. When I refused to say anything and denied it all, I was accused of lying. He was going to be taken down, at least that's what law enforcement reminded me.

I thought the best thing for me to do was attend church and work on myself. By now, I had started to isolate myself from friends. I was the quiet one... possibly slightly nerdy. But even the church, the one place I thought would be safe, betrayed me. The very place I thought I would be safe. The place of worship. The place where you can connect to the Lord himself. I devoted myself to youth ministry, preaching about what God had done for us. One night, I was the last one for one of the guys to drop off. He took me to the parking lot of an elementary school and started to get sexual with me. When I told my aunt, she did what anyone else would have done: she told the Pastor. The only problem was that they wanted to confront us all together. The night of the confrontation, before I walked into the room, the guy was waiting for me by these stairs, and demanded I follow him. I was so scared because I didn't know what he was going to do. He begged me not to say anything because he could lose his privileges. This is when I realized I would have to defend men for their actions ...even when they were wrong. So I did as he asked me. Why? Because it was also that way with my uncle. Even with the restraining order. My family kept him around, and if anything, pushed me away as a liar. And since this was the case, I remember thinking how the church would be no different if they brought me here with this man, with him demanding that I not say a word. Who was ever going to protect me? That night confirmed what I had always feared, whether in family or in faith. I would always be left unprotected.

I was the laughing-stock after that. The liar. I ruined people's lives. And this is where I made the mistake of looking for love and protection. Going into high school, I was still alone. I didn't know many of the students in this school, since my mom didn't want me to go to the school that all my friends were going to. Welcome to the Vikings, Westhill High School. This is where I met more Hispanic kids and got labeled as a wannabe American. How confusing. My family didn't want me, and these kids teased me. "Fresh meat," most of the boys said. Well, my American accent and my vaccination shot from having dual citizenship confused the hell out of them. Just another place for me to feel like

I didn't belong. Then I started hanging out with friends, and that is where I met my first ex-husband.

I started sneaking out, going to clubs, drinking, and being with people who were much older than me. My mom had no idea how troubled I was. I don't blame her, though. She went through life working as a housekeeper all day, paying my uncle's bonds from money she borrowed from loan sharks. We were broke, and my mom never sought help. She was occupied by the family she was taught to take care of. And then, one day, I was pregnant. Pregnant at 15. I remember how much I rubbed my belly and made the promise of protecting her. Promising to give her all the love I had needed from my own mother. Love, time, kindness, gentleness, and protection. I was published by the New York Times on how I wanted other kids to protect themselves and wait to have children. The cost of having children that young was difficult. We had two kids together and then split up when I realized we wanted different things in life.

He wanted a wife who would sit and watch him drink on the weekends. I wanted the white picket fence with the beautiful family and home. As life continued, I realized I was too broken. I felt lost and unlovable.

I finally met my biological father when I was almost 18. An "adult" with two kids. He is nothing but the #1 piece of shit. He raped me. I came home one night from dinner with my girlfriends. My body was no longer mine. I couldn't move. I fought to open my eyes and felt like I was losing myself. Was I dying? I remember feeling like I shouldn't have survived that night. He violated every inch of me. He destroyed every single feeling I had. Luckily, he's in one of the maximum prisons in Connecticut, thanks to the detective who picked him up when he re-entered the country. He had run out of the States when there were charges presented against him for doing the same to another minor child. The problem is, the person he did this to didn't deserve it. It was my daughter. Had I spoken up when it happened to me, I could have saved my baby. Instead, I chose to stay quiet. Thinking, if no one believed me before, then who would believe me now? I ended up closing down. I shut out everyone I could. I distanced myself from it all and protected my kids.

By doing this, I no longer associated with my own family. I tried dating, and it was hard. I had two kids at a young age, and the guys I met were just wanting to drink, go out, and party. I couldn't keep up. I wasn't the fittest, the prettiest, or a fashionista like most women. My confidence was extremely low. I started working in the car business. I tried my best to figure out how to make more money and lift my kids out of this lifestyle.

Poverty is extremely common for most kids with teen pregnancies, and I was one of them. I was able to start as an office assistant at a small dealership; this is where I learned I had a passion for accounting. I realized that organizing and managing the accounts was easy. I picked up the rules and started reading up on my own about Profit & Loss, balance sheets, and how the journal entries connected to one another. I loved not having to talk to anyone, especially after sales. But then it happened there, too. The man was married. He argued with his wife often, and I never understood why. Until one day, he yelled at me and told me his wife was arguing with him, thinking he had something going on with me. That's when he put his hand down my shirt and said if he is going to get accused of something, he might as well do it. My best friend had started working there; I never told her or anyone. But one day, I couldn't handle it anymore, so I quit.

I ended up working somewhere else where I felt safe, seen, and valuable. I never heard of him again. Looking back, if it wasn't for my best friend working there, I don't know how much worse it could have been. But I was lucky. The only problem was I didn't feel complete there, either. I missed my kids so much. I worked long hours, and I was grateful for the opportunity. Working with Lexus of Greenwich showed me what semi-corporate looks like. Other organizations gave me so much growth and confidence. I met some people that I valued so much that I was truly thankful for. The one I remember the most was an older gentleman named Joe. He always brought me a little note with the Bible verse for that day and always made sure I got them.

But I needed more. An old friend of mine lived in Wilson, NC. I fell in love with the area, and it looked family-oriented. While I was considering the move, I was introduced to my second ex-husband. There were so many signs that I should have turned away and run for my dear life. He knew exactly what to say to me. The first sign was that he was with another woman, and how he treated her when she wasn't around. At 25, you're still naïve. He told me they had only been dating for 2 weeks, and it wasn't working out. He had brought her to my then-friend's birthday. She said some questionable things when I met her. Not that it was my business, because at that time, I thought he was just another wanna be fuckboy with the attitude he showed. For some reason, she wanted to show how he was doing things for her. I wanted to yell and tell her, "Good for you! I hope you prosper in life." This man pursued me, claiming I was everything he had searched for in a woman. We flew to NYC one weekend, where he wined and dined me.

The beginning of what I thought was love quickly turned into a cycle of control, fear, and violence. That relationship unearthed so many triggers tied to the trauma I had endured before; it forced me to face the darkest parts of myself. Even in the middle of all the pain, I knew I had to keep fighting for myself and for my kids. Family always meant the world to me, and yet, at every stage, I felt torn away from those who were supposed to be there for me. Healing wasn't immediate, and being vulnerable needed more strength than I had ever imagined. Working through the layers of trauma, from childhood to adulthood, gave me the strength to rebuild. The journey of survival, reflection, and growth led me not only to a successful career path but to the healthiest, most supportive relationship of my life. I am living proof that even after all the storms, there can be peace, purpose, and love on the other side.

To every woman who has walked through fire and still questions her worth, know that survival itself is proof of your strength. We are often taught to shrink, to silence ourselves, or to accept less than we deserve, but there is power in reclaiming our story. Your scars are not signs of weakness; they are reminders that you endured what was meant to break you. There is no shame in the process of healing, no matter how long it takes. What matters is that you continue to rise. Your resilience becomes the light that guides others out of their own darkness.

We can go over all the things that worked for me and all the trauma I faced, but the reality is that what you face will always be your own, and the way we heal comes at different times and stages of our lives. My advice: love yourself so deeply that you create the strength to pour love into others, and allow yourself the grace to be fully yourself in return.

ABOUT THE AUTHOR

Allison Banegas is a finance professional and writer whose strength was forged through survival and healing. Her chapter in Split reflects the deeply personal journey of a woman who rebuilt her life after domestic violence and not by forgetting the past, but by transforming it into purpose.

Allison's story is one of courage, motherhood, and renewal. Through pain, she discovered the resilience that comes from self acceptance and the quiet power of choosing peace over fear. Her voice now stands as a reminder that healing is not linear, but it is possible and that every woman has the right to safety, dignity, and a love that does not hurt.

Connect:
   Instagram @allyyvane
   Facebook @Ally Banegas
   TikTok @allyvane
   Threads @allyyvane

CHAPTER 10

Faith in the Fire

JEN KENNEDY, MPA

To Landon and Charlotte, the great loves of my life.

I woke up the morning of my wedding not knowing if I would be getting married that day. Why? Two days earlier, my groom's excessive drinking at his bachelor party had sent him to the ER with severe dehydration. He was physically unable to stand for more than a few minutes and had to sit through much of the wedding rehearsal and rehearsal dinner. I went to bed that night, unsure if he would even be physically able to participate in the wedding. Should that have been a red flag? Maybe? Was it going to deter me from marrying him? Definitely NOT! I was a child of the *Happily Ever After (HEA)* generation; love would conquer all, and any issues we had during dating would magically disappear as we floated off into newlywedded bliss.

I was and am a woman of faith; a devout Christian who has lived her life believing in, and sustained by, a faith that told me I was so much more than the child who grew up in a home of domestic violence, a victim who suffered physical, emotional, psychological, sexual abuse and assault inside and outside the home as a teenager moving into adulthood. I saw my new husband and his happily married Christian parents as the golden ticket that guaranteed a happy life. I believed that by choosing a man who shared my faith, I was entering into a union that would be blessed with happiness and love. Sure, I knew that there would be challenges, but the first quarter century of my life had already been so hard, so many things to overcome, that this marriage just had to be my time for a home filled with joy, faith, comfort and safety. That, however, was not what happened, due in large part to not only some of my ex-husband's choices, but mine - I, at times, was absolutely the villain in my supposed HEA.

Looking back on my marriage, it would be easy to simply point fingers, minimize my villainous activities while calling out a laundry list of grievances against my ex. That, however, is not what you came here for. I wanted to write this chapter because I wanted to share some of the faith, hope and love that found me, followed me, surrounded me, and strengthened me as I walked through fifteen years of trying to make my marriage work. In the end, it was that same faith, hope, and love that released me.

Going back to that bride, the morning of her wedding, the drama of the rehearsal was not the first red flag of my relationship with my ex-husband. Shortly before he proposed, I learned that my then-boyfriend of 11 months liked to gamble. We lived in Las Vegas. I knew he gambled, that he enjoyed it, and by all appearances, had some talent at it. Talent enough, I thought, for no consequences other than the occasional spa day comped for me and chip winnings found tucked into random pockets. What I did not know was that at times, the amount he gambled was more than I realized, and having grown up in a home that was not much above the poverty line, it was significantly more than I was comfortable with.

After finding out about a series of wins and losses that I hadn't known about, I urged my now fiancée to consider talking to someone, and asked him if this was something to be concerned about. Assurances were given, fears were calmed, and in the true spirit of a princess finding her prince, I forged ahead with wedding plans and what my HEA was going to look like, unconcerned.

About 18 months later, after learning about another series of wins and losses that threatened the tenuous stability I felt I/we were trying to build for our future, I began contemplating divorce. I was afraid, didn't understand why I had such a problem with his gambling, and didn't know how I was supposed to cope. Overwhelmed, I drove home from work, loud thoughts in the silence of the car, my mind racing at what to do, when I heard a voice. An audible voice filled my car, and a voice gently but firmly told me, "Stay with your husband, give Me time."

To this day, I can tell you where I was on my neighborhood street when I heard that voice, the sight of the trees, desert landscaping and quiet, older homes, the backdrop for a moment I had prayed for countless times over the course of my life. I knew with absolute certainty that the voice I heard was the voice of God. I knew from the depths of my soul that God was instructing me to stay with my husband, that He had a plan for me, and He needed me to stay the course.

My reaction? Anger. Nothing but a pure surge of fire in my veins. I was so unbelievably mad at God; driving through my neighborhood to my house, and into the garage of the home we had purchased only six months prior, I told God in no uncertain terms how angry I was with Him. I like to imagine that to my Heavenly Father, I probably looked more like a hissing little cat than a righteously angry, formidable woman, but that was how I saw myself. I was outraged. I had grown up in abuse, been raped, sexually assaulted in college (and ostracized for reporting it), had two parents with serious mental health conditions, had *begged* God to show himself to me, speak to me, comfort me more times than I could count, and it FINALLY happens ...and it is about my HUSBAND?!?!

To be honest, I think words my army parents may have forgotten they ever repeated in front of me poured out of my mouth, completely unfiltered, as I raged and cried, feeling despair, envy, resentment and a host of other emotions equal in both their intensity and complexity. When that storm of emotions passed, I was neither settled nor at peace. I was still angry, still jealous that God talked to me about my husband, and not about ME. I was the one whose life had practically been a trial by fire; why was I hearing about him?

But I was determined to be faithful; after talking with the Associate Pastor of my church and his wife, who led the young married couple's group we attended, I began to accept that God had a better plan for me than I could understand, and all I was being asked to do was to walk in faith. That fire of anger and frustration that coursed through my body didn't disappear, but instead transformed into hot embers of determination. If God was telling me to stay, remain faithful in the fire, I was determined to obey. So walk in faith, I did....

Through the blessings and challenges of two healthy children (an older boy and a younger girl, just as I always prayed for), undiagnosed post-partum depression with my son, and diagnosed post-partum depression with my daughter.

Through disagreements about everything from finances, diapers, parenting responsibilities, and the division of chores, while both of us held full-time careers.

Through my going back to school for my Master's degree, fishing trips, hunting adventures, shared awe at the miracle that was our children, therapy for me for anger and anxiety, therapy for him, marriage counseling together and separately.

Through my parents' eventual divorce after basically 20 years of separation, my heartbreaking decision to finally cut ties with my dad to stop the emotional abuse I had continued to allow into adulthood, and my father's eventual death at his own hands.

Through a seemingly endless blur of debates and fights over my husband's choice to gamble and our diverging views on the subject.

I walked in faith through the fire.

I cried, I raged, I laughed, I worried, I prayed, I loved, and tried to understand how the world kept calmly rotating on its axis while I felt my world spinning uncontrollably like a possessed carnival ride I could not get off of. With each experience, each heartbreak and challenge, I would remember that God had spoken to me, asked me to have faith, to give Him time, so I did.

Eventually, my husband came to me and told me he no longer felt like Las Vegas was the best place for our family. Between the hot desert climate, the gambling, and the desire for our children to experience a different life, he asked if we could consider moving somewhere different. I was 100% opposed at the start. I liked my job, we had family in the area, our children were attending a good school, and to be honest, I felt like I finally had a strong group of girlfriends, and I did not want to give up any of that. He persisted, however, and to appease him, I went ahead and applied for one job in Washington....ONE JOB.

Imagine my surprise when, one video interview later, I got a phone call from the HR manager saying that they were offering me the job. Needless to say, I was not amused. I did not want to move! I sat outside on a bench, looking at the grass amphitheater at work, wondering how I even got a job when I only participated in one video interview. Didn't they at least want to meet me in person? A few days later, as I sat at home thinking about the offer, I realized that taking this job was very simply just continuing my practice of walking in faith, of seeing where God was opening a door for me to walk through.

Once again, I found myself struggling with feelings of frustration and even anger - I did NOT want to move, I did NOT want to be obedient to God's will. However, I knew from some spectacularly challenging moments in my life that ignoring God, not being obedient... well, it didn't end well for me. Therefore, it felt prudent to obey, so I accepted the job and agreed to move. I did have one stipulation, however, and that was that if we moved and my husband continued to gamble, it might not necessarily be the end of our marriage, but if he was not honest about his activities or hid his gambling, I could not, and would not continue in our marriage.

I wish I could say that with the move we left our problems behind us, but anywhere we move, we (the collective we) are still there. In Washington, like Las Vegas, there were casinos and betting opportunities. While he sometimes bet when he went back to Las Vegas, it seemed that he respected my boundary while he was in Washington. Sadly, almost 14 months after our move, I learned my husband had been gambling in Washington.

For me, this was a huge problem, because that was simply not an activity I wanted in my life. I'll never forget sitting on the bed in our room, looking at my husband, a sick feeling twisting my stomach into knots until I felt like I was going to throw up. The sadness and resignation on his face as he asked me, "What are you going to do?"

I took a deep breath and replied, "I honestly don't know, I really don't."

In that moment, I realized that although I had set a boundary, a line in the sand, one I expected him to follow, I had not emotionally prepared myself for that follow-through. There was only one clear thought in my head: "Well, shit – what the actual fuck am I going to do now!?"

As I drove to work that morning and sat at my desk, I felt as though I was suffocating. My skin felt hot and tight, the pressure on my chest, with each inhale burning from what felt like smoke stealing the very breath from my lungs. I had only one clear thought: "I need to pray."

So with the focus and determination that had guided me through so many challenges in the past, I walked in faith. I prayed, talked to my therapist (who was also a Christian), cried and prayed some more, had emotional and deeply healing moments with friends and family who understood the importance of my faith and obedience. For almost a month, I existed in this limbo, uncertain of what to do, what more I could handle, what responsibilities I had to my children, my husband, and myself.

About a month after my discovery, I got my answer. I had been praying while in the shower, letting my tears be washed away by the water, as I asked God for help and guidance. As I got out of the shower, I heard a voice - this time in my heart–that said:

"See, when I said give Me more time, I was not just talking about your husband, I was saying give Me time for YOU."

Then, the Lord showed me what He meant. He showed me that I had a job that allowed me financial independence (albeit potentially dependent on PB&J lunches and Top Ramen dinners), and bosses who were amazingly supportive and compassionate. I had built some strong, beautiful friendships in Washington while still cultivating relationships with friends in Las Vegas. I belonged to a vibrant and lively church, and my children were happy and thriving both in the classroom and with their own friendships.

In essence, for the first time in my adult life, God was showing me that I could split from the life I knew and be able to take care of myself and my children. Every move, every choice, every moment of obedience had allowed me to walk through the flames, along a path that God had laid out, without being burned. It had been hot, uncomfortably so, but God had made a way through the fire when I chose to walk in faith.

I knew God was telling me it was time for me to move out of the way, to allow Him to work on my husband in ways I could not, just as

He was working on me in ways my husband could not. I feel as strongly today as I did that fateful February day that God was releasing me from my marriage. So I chose to walk in faith....and told my husband it was time to separate and divorce.

It was utterly devastating. As soul-crushingly lonely as moments of my marriage had been, this was a thousand times worse. I knew that I was going to hurt our children, our families, myself and yes, my husband. I was desperate not to hurt anyone, and would have sacrificed myself if I could have kept from hurting any of them, but in my heart I knew that God was telling me to move out of the way, that it was time to step aside.

There must have been a decisiveness in my tone and demeanor when I told my husband it was over, because there was no argument, not even a whisper of protest. It was as if he knew instinctively that this time was different, I was different, my motivations were different. This wasn't me yelling, threatening or trying to force something. This was a quiet whisper of finality to my words, a commitment to change the course of our lives, the acknowledgement of a split that could not be repaired.

And with that conversation, my imagined Happily Ever After was over. My life had been reduced to ashes, no longer resembling the hopes and dreams I had once had. Divorce, even when it brings relief, is painful, the kind of pain that burns so hot, so fast, your nerves are completely obliterated. Late at night, though, your nerves begin to regain feeling, pulses of pain to wake you, beating in time with your broken heart as tears slip from your eyes onto your pillow and you struggle to breathe through the pain and the grief.

Life continues, though; I have learned these last two years that each step by painful step, taken in obedience, moves me in the direction of the life that God wants for me. Yes, I was obedient in staying in my marriage, and yes, I was obedient in ending my marriage, but that does not mean my journey is over, nor is my need to walk in faith. There have been countless moments where I have felt the fire all around me, challenging and reshaping me, forging in me a new strength with every step I take.

I once thought my HEA revolved around a husband, a family, a princess-like dream. I now know, though, that it comes from my walking in faith and obedience to God. My Happily Ever After is something that will come from my relationship with God, built on faith and trust. Because the God who has seen me through so many fires is the God who walks with me now. Knowing that, believing that, regardless of what trial by fire I find myself in, I am able to continue to walk step by step and have faith in the midst of the fire.

ABOUT THE AUTHOR

Jen Kennedy has a Masters in Public Administration and works as a senior management analyst for a utility company, so she is able to have adventures with her children and support Luna and Pebbles treat addictions!

Formerly of Las Vegas, Nevada, Jen enjoys taking full advantage of the PNW's gorgeous weather to engage in her hobbies of hiking, biking, and, best of all, running (even in the rain). Her other passions include quality time with family and friends, exploring new food spots and local cider houses, and growing in her relationship with Christ as He guides her through this chapter of her life.

Connect:
www.linkedin.com/in/jen-kennedy-mpa-a7b77814

CHAPTER 11
I Never Belonged to One World

LATOYA BURDISS

I have never belonged to one world entirely. Instead, I have always lived in the spaces between them.

I have always lived in the middle. The middle shade on the color chart; too light to be Black, too brown to be white. In many ways, our world thinks in halves: half Black, half white. Half of a household. Half of a couple. I know far too well what happens when none of your halves match. You learn to claim yourself. You learn to speak fluently in contradiction and become the translator at every table, all to make the pieces fit. Those who may not understand might see living a split life as a daunting task. But for me, it was a game of push and pull, a means of survival.

I never really cared why my father was not there; it never occurred to me that I was missing out. In my mind, there was nothing my mom couldn't do, and the idea of me needing to depend on another never crossed my mind. Ironically, I did not feel surrounded by kids with two parents in their homes. So I never thought of mine as different. It was not until my late thirties that I realized there was something missing from living in that middle space.

Holidays were divided occasions. Mornings and afternoons with my mother's family; evenings with my father's. Looking back, I realize I held on to childlike assumptions and questions I never asked. My father would pick me up, sometimes at six, sometimes at eight. I used to think, Black people must just eat dinner late. Only later did I realize everyone had already eaten. My father was not late because of culture; he was just late.

And though I knew they were my kin, I often felt like a misfit. I did not know how to play Bid Whist, but I loved listening to the laughter, the shouts of "uptown!" and "downtown!", the rhythm of belonging wrapped in cards and good trash talk. Spades, though, I could play. I could slap my Big Joker down with pride, claiming my space in the family puzzle. But when the night ended, so did the connection. The next holiday was my reset. There were no slamming cards or dominoes once I crossed back into my other life.

I did not know I was different from my classmates until someone told me. It happened in fragments, each one carving away at my sense of belonging. In second grade, Brooke gave me an invitation to her birthday party, along with everyone else in the class. But the invitation came with a warning: "I really want you to come, but if you did, my dad would shoot you." In seventh grade, students thought it was funny to label the water fountains for "Whites" and "Coloreds." My dance club advisor, my English teacher, told staff in the break room that I was her "good little n***r" who handled all the club duties.

Split at home. Split at school. My spirit—split.

School itself was split, too. There was the academic side, where I knew I could excel, and the social side, where I was a chameleon, able to blend in even when I did not fully belong. My grandmother used to say, "You were two years old reading the newspaper." But by first grade, I was placed in a Slingerland class. I did not know what that meant; I just knew I was different.

I remember tracing letters in the air, feeling confusion rise in my small chest. I was not there long. By second grade, I was being tested for the gifted program. My IQ was over 140. I skipped third grade, catching up with the kids I had already befriended. Years later, I learned Slingerland was designed for students with dyslexia. I still wonder why I was placed there? Was it because I was too dark? Because my name was on the free lunch list? Because someone assumed split meant broken?

I spent most of my life trying to fit my reflection into someone else's frame. My skin tone was a puzzle piece no one could quite place. "What are you?" they would ask, as if I were a riddle to be solved. Then they would ask, "Where are you from?". The look on their faces when I replied that I was born and raised in Anchorage, Alaska, was a combination of bewilderment and curiosity. I don't know if people were expecting a southern drawl or maybe even a Polynesian island as my answer. Instead, they got snow, and I got silence.

Growing up in Anchorage meant living surrounded by vastness, darkness, and isolation. The only brightness was brought about from the snow. Winters lasted long enough to make you forget what color looked like, and the summers went by so fast it was as if you were to blink, you would miss it. I did not realize then how much the landscape mirrored me. Every six months we knew what to expect. The days went from shadows to shining. Alaska was not the place most people pictured when they saw me. But it was home, even if belonging there always felt like something I had to explain.

What am I supposed to look like? I was too much of one thing and not enough of another. My face made people guess; my voice made them assume. When I smiled, someone always said, "You look just like your mom." When I frowned, they would insist, "You've got your daddy's eyes." But no one ever saw me, just the halves that made me palatable to whichever side was more comfortable.

For years, I measured my worth by who decided to claim me that day. White spaces treated me like a diversity statement; Black spaces tested my legitimacy. The mirrors I stood before reflected only partial truths. And so I learned to live between them, to occupy the hyphen, to make the middle my home.

Maybe I am not half of anything. Maybe I am the sum of everything that refuses to divide.

Love, too, was another kind of split. The kind that smiled in photos and trembled in pews.

When I fell in love with her, it was not rebellion; it was recognition. She was the first person who looked at me and did not see halves, only whole. We said yes. We said love. We said forever.

But they said no. No to the wedding invitation. No to the marriage certificate that carried both our names. No to the idea that our love could coexist with their God.

Some called it sin. Others called it confusion. I called it home.

In the same breath, I learned how affirmation and erasure could coexist, how love could be both sanctuary and spotlight. At work, I was "brave" for being out. At church, I was "welcomed," but only if I left part of myself at the door. Love was the great mirror that showed me not only who I was but who the world refused to see.

It is strange how love can both heal and expose the places you did not know were still raw.

Faith was my first language, spoken before I knew the sound of my own uncertainty. I was not raised on hymns and hallelujahs, or prayers whispered over everything from dinner to report cards. But as a young adult, I tried the idea of church as a place of refuge, and I found that some sanctuaries have doors that only open one way.

When I came out, I did not leave my faith. My faith left me. Or maybe it was taken. People said they loved me, but their love came with fine print: You can sit here, but not serve there. You can worship, but not lead.

It is a peculiar kind of grief to mourn the idea of a God you thought existed.

Still, I found faith in unexpected places. I found it in friends who accepted me without trying to change me and in quiet moments of gratitude. Maybe grace was never meant to be confined to walls or doctrines. Maybe the divine, too, lives in the in-between.

We don't always see the unraveling while it is happening. Sometimes, it is just the quiet turning of threads loosening one by one.

When my marriage ended, there was no explosion. No slammed doors or shouted goodbyes. Just silence, a steady exhale of something that had been held too tightly for too long.

Divorce is another kind of split. The one that forces you to confront the pieces of yourself you've ignored. I realized how long I had been performing togetherness while feeling alone. How much of me had been invested in proving I could make something whole out of fragments.

I thought love would fix the fracture. It did not. It just revealed how deep it went. And my inability to use my voice allowed the downward spiral to affect me in ways I did not know was possible.

Since our split, I met myself again: raw, unsure, but honest. There is a kind of mercy in starting over, in stripping away the layers that never belonged to you in the first place.

The middle used to feel like torment. Now it feels like possibility.

I am the child of a single mother. The daughter of distance. The product of Black and white, of faith and doubt, of love and letting go. I am what happens when a split life learns to stand on its own.

School taught me how to survive. Love is teaching me how to live.

Maybe I'll never fit neatly into one category. Maybe I was never meant to. Because being split did not destroy me, it revealed me.

I am not half of anything. I am the sum of everything I have carried, everything I have lost, and everything I am still becoming.

And maybe this is not just my story. Maybe "split" is what connects us all, the fault lines that shape our becoming; and perhaps healing lives in the middle, where contradictions stop fighting and start coexisting. Or maybe, split is not broken after all. Maybe it is just all the pieces finally learning to live together.

ABOUT THE AUTHOR

LaToya Burdiss is a higher education professional and doctoral researcher at an institution of higher education. She oversees recreational programs and leads initiatives that promote student engagement, leadership, and well-being. With more than a decade of experience in program management and student development, she focuses on helping students find their place, build confidence, and discover what success looks like for them.

Her doctoral research examines suicidality among U.S. undergraduate students, with a focus on prevention, intervention, and the institutional factors that influence well-being in higher education. LaToya integrates evidence-based practices and developmental theory into her work, aligning academic insight with real-world application to enhance campus culture and student support systems.

Committed to lifelong learning and community impact, she also contributes to leadership and professional development programming, curriculum design, and staff mentorship. Her work reflects a passion for cultivating spaces where students and professionals can thrive both personally and collectively.

Connect:
www.facebook.com/latoya.burdiss
www.instagram.com/burdissl
www.linkedin.com/in/latoya-burdiss-a7ab239

CHAPTER 12
Living a Lie
CHRISTEN E. BRYCE, MS, RN

Pregnant at 23, my world seemed to crumble around me. Twenty years later, it seems like a lifetime ago, but it still feels like yesterday. Within four months, I endured three of the most earth-shattering changes that I had ever experienced up to that point in my life (albeit the birth of my daughter was a positive one). Little did I know that a few months after my beautiful, healthy, "miracle baby" was born, I would be overcome with both the grief of my grandfather's death and that of my parents' shocking divorce (after almost 25 years of marriage).

It was as if my whole world was exploding like a soda bottle that had been vigorously shaken, thrown on the floor, and then opened upside down over my head. All I could think at the time was, *"My whole life has been a lie,"* and that it had happened almost overnight. Eventually, I learned that what I once viewed as lies could be turned into life lessons and silver linings.

He was not just some one-night stand. He wasn't even a fling. He was my boyfriend for just under three years. The boyfriend I thought I had a future with. We'd certainly had our ups and downs, had even broken up for a few months the year before. We had supported each other through some difficulties during college, and both of us transferred to schools closer to home for our final year. However, when I found out that I was pregnant, I very quickly learned that you can love a person and not actually know what they're capable of.

The shock of this pregnancy was intensified because of my own internal conflict—a "devout Catholic" who had relations outside of marriage—it was like I had been lying to myself *and* everyone around me. Everyone who knew me, who saw me in church, would now know the truth about how I'd had sex and gotten pregnant by some loser boyfriend who decided he didn't feel like taking responsibility.

He wrote in an email that he didn't want to have a baby who would eventually "emulate his actions." Which actions, exactly? I'm not quite sure, because I have never spoken to him again in my life. All I could assume he meant by that statement was that we were only 23 and he still loved drinking and partying too much to be bothered with taking on the responsibilities and roles required of a father. I am quite certain that he was on the way to becoming an alcoholic. He had shared with me that his own father walked out on their family when he was seven years old. He had caught his father in the act, cheating on his mother, and had told me his father had been an alcoholic. Perhaps he felt that if he left while I was pregnant, he wouldn't risk the possibility of abandoning us later, as his own father had done to his wife and child. But, this is all speculation; I will never know what he actually meant by that statement. All I knew at the time was that having a pregnant belly as a single mom with no "baby daddy" would be like wearing a sign on my forehead that says, "I had sex with a deadbeat asshole." The guilt was unbearable.

The real kicker was that while all of this was going on with me, another relationship was about to end, and there would be no beautiful, healthy baby girl as the silver lining at the end of *that* tunnel. My parents, who had always seemed like the "perfect" middle-class couple–even to me and my siblings–told us while I was pregnant that they had been miserable for years, and would be separating once my sister turned 18.

Never once did I see them fight when I was growing up. Mild bickering, perhaps, but they kept their disagreements private (apparently). I guess it was naive of us to think that they just had a "perfect marriage". Perfect does not exist. We had still been going on family vacations, doing the same family holiday traditions, hosting family parties, and we had been the "hang out house" for our friends even through college. We lived very comfortably; most importantly, we were raised with an unwavering faith in God. I truly thought that we were a happy, strong family. I remember always feeling so sad for the kids who grew up with divorced parents. That was unimaginable; I *knew* that would never happen to me.

But no. Lies. Everything I had believed or strived to become up until that moment was breaking apart. Traditions were BROKEN. Family parties became NON-EXISTENT. Trust was GONE.

Instead of bringing my baby into an intact family, my first few years of navigating motherhood were often spent questioning whether I'd ever know what a "healthy" marriage is. I began questioning whether marriage would ever be in my own future. My life became a mix of emotions—loneliness, awkwardness, indescribable sadness, anger, and resentment—all while experiencing the most pure and unconditional love, excitement, gratitude, and joy as a brand new single mom to my daughter. How does one handle the loss of a boyfriend, a grandfather, and an intact nuclear family all at once? With a little defense mechanism known as suppression.

Fast forward to 2013. I got married in January and had my second daughter in December. Looking back now, I realize how much my parents' divorce had affected my ability to pick a mate, my trust of others, and my overall mental health. I never healed from one grief before I was hit with another one.

My own marriage went sour faster than the Eras Tour sold out. Our communication skills were so horrendous that we could barely be in the same house without arguing. After three YEARS of marriage counseling, and way too much emotional damage for my already fatherless daughter to handle, we decided to start the divorce process. We attempted to live together for three months while beginning the process of separation, but it quickly became unbearable. If you have ever wondered what it feels like when someone says, "you could cut the air with a knife," you would have immediately understood it when you walked in our front door. I made the decision to protect my girls from living in such a toxic environment, and we went to temporarily live with my mom. Our youngest went back and forth, but my oldest daughter stayed with me 100% of the time.

Prior to my leaving, he and I had tried mediation for a day, but the things that were said to the mediator were not the same things that were being said to me at home. I also discovered that he had hired an attorney without my knowledge. Not just any attorney, but through a firm in our area known specifically for "father's rights." From that point, I lived at an anxiety level of 10/10 and feared what his next moves would be every single day for a year, until we had a written agreement in place, and the divorce was finalized. We did manage to avoid a full trial... at least at that point in our lives. However, I'd be lying if I told you that things improved after the divorce was finalized. For years, co-parenting was minimal, and everything continued to be a fight.

"Great," I'd think to myself. *"Second generation of a divorced family, my girls will be a mess, and I haven't even healed from my own past."*

My marriage truly was one that, in my opinion, could not have ever lasted or been repaired. Sometimes I'm not even sure how we ended up together in the first place. We are such different people, with different life goals and values. But even if we had been more compatible, I know that I was bringing an undeniable fear into any relationship I had. The slightest turmoil would lead me to think that it would be better not to drag it out by staying together for years, like my parents did. All I knew was how fucked up *I* felt after my parents' late-life ("grey") divorce. Every time we would argue or fight, I'd find myself saying that I would rather get divorced when our daughter was two, so that she would not grow up in a toxic environment. She wouldn't even remember us being married. All she would ever know is that she has two loving parents who are happily and healthily living apart. And let me tell you...I'm sure glad I followed my gut on that. However, living as a divorced child and going back and forth is just as shitty in its own way; I am not at all downplaying that. But at least she will not grow up thinking that our marriage is what marriage should look like.

Something very negative became a huge life lesson, strengthening my faith in God and in myself. My confidence, mindset and ability to fully put my trust in God improved more than I ever dreamed they could. Do I still find myself feeling defeated, anxious, and flat-out depressed sometimes? Of course! But how I handle my stress has made me an overall healthier person, a better mom for my kids, and despite everything, I have been able to heal in ways I never thought were possible!

Sadly, as adults, we get all wrapped up in our own issues, whether it's during a divorce or not. Kids notice everything. They see our emotions, feel our moods, hear our fights and negative comments. As parents, we need to be mindful of every little remark, sarcastic comment, every eye roll we make in their presence—no matter how old they are. We can't leave them behind or ignore their requests. Know that acting out can be a direct result of what they see, feel, hear, and experience. Their brains are still developing. They may not know how to put their thoughts into words. I recall the insane tantrums my toddler had while we were divorcing. Sure, some of it had to do with "normal toddler stuff," but looking back, I know that it was also her way of being pissed off. She surely couldn't understand why she wasn't seeing mommy *and* daddy every day. When children are adults at the time of divorce, they may still "act out," just in very different ways.

Divorce is a life-altering and emotionally taxing experience that profoundly affects both parents and children, regardless of age. Over the past few decades, late-life divorce has risen sharply, especially among couples married for over 20 years. From 1990 to 2022, divorces among couples aged 55 and older doubled, while those for couples 65 and older tripled. This phenomenon has become known as "grey" divorce, coined by Susan Brown and I-Fen Lin in their 2012 study. Despite these undeniable statistics, there continues to be a lack of acknowledgement and streamlined support for the unique grief and destruction that late-life divorce can cause for families.

While waiting until the children are older to end a marriage may seem like the "easier" or "better" option for one reason or another, the adult children of grey divorce (ACOGD) might disagree. The pain, hurt, confusion, and anger that come along with the dissolution of a family don't magically disappear at a certain age. Very few studies have looked specifically at how grey divorce affects the psychological well-being and interpersonal relationships of ACOGD. It's almost like ACOGD is a "forgotten population."

Have *you* ever heard someone say they stayed (or are staying) together "for the kids?" It's a familiar sentiment, and perhaps you've even seen it play out in your own family. As I expressed at the beginning of the chapter regarding my own experience, when divorce occurs between one's parents, the world is essentially turned upside down, no matter the age. The shock for all involved, and sudden upheaval of family traditions can be just as intense—if not more so—when it occurs later in life. We need to remember that every single situation and individual dealing with it is like a fingerprint - no two are exactly alike.

Oftentimes, if the "children" are adults themselves, they are expected or assumed to be able to handle the changes maturely; the reality of their feelings may even get pushed aside or go unrecognized. They are left to navigate through some or all of the stages of grief: shock, denial, anger, bargaining, depression, testing, and acceptance. Most likely, they will struggle with mixed feelings such as betrayal, sadness, resentment, and confusion. *These emotions may manifest immediately or be suppressed, like mine were, until years later when they can resurface as fear of commitment, self-doubt, self-loathing, and distrust of others.* Without proper healing, any type of grief can become a full-blown mental illness, like depression, anxiety, or substance abuse. ACOGD are unfortunately at an increased risk for their own marriages to end in divorce, making it even more important for them to have access to resources and support specifically tailored to them and their needs.

Growing up in what seemed like a "healthy" family created a sense of security for me. As children reach young adulthood with their parents still married, they often feel invincible—safe from the possibility of divorce disrupting their world. That's why the shock an adult child feels upon hearing that their parents are separating after years of marriage can be unimaginable. In these moments, adult children are often expected to stay composed and independent, even as their family structure crumbles before their eyes. While young children are often seen as more vulnerable to divorce, adult children feel equally destabilized and shaken as the foundation they thought was secure. Questioning the validity of my entire identity and childhood was something I grappled with alone is something that I sat alone with for years.

The common societal assumption that adult children are less affected by their parents' divorce than younger children has, in my opinion, partially led to my feelings of loneliness. People often fail to acknowledge how this life-altering event can forever disrupt the bonds built over decades, as parents and children adjust to a new, unfamiliar dynamic. What people may not think about until they personally go through something like this is that grey divorce often flips social roles within the family structure. Adult children are suddenly expected to comfort one or both parents instead of receiving support themselves. Some parents, overwhelmed by stress, may overlook their grown children's needs, assuming they're less affected because they're adults. This unintentional insensitivity can leave adult children feeling unseen as they navigate their grief, further complicating the healing process. Parents often believe that divorce is harder on younger children, assuming their grown children will understand and accept the decision. The grief they experience is often unacknowledged, without adequate support. Sometimes this alone can lead to even more strain on parent-child relationships.

Although grey divorce brings about significant emotional changes and challenges within families, it also presents opportunities for resilience and growth. Families can rebuild healthier relationships, and adult children can develop stronger coping mechanisms as they navigate the shifts in their family dynamic. This resilience can lead to newfound strength and understanding within relationships moving forward. It just comes down to finding the right process, resources, and support.

Navigating grief, whether from your own or your parents' divorce later in life, can feel overwhelming. Over the years, I've unintentionally applied the following steps to my own life and coined it as *The C.R.I.S.I.S. Plan*. This plan provides a clear starting point for you to pivot when faced with emotional turmoil and immediately begin implementing the steps in a way that can be molded to fit your life.

According to the APA Dictionary of Psychology (2018), a crisis can be defined as *anything that produces significant cognitive or emotional stress for those involved*. Personal crises are subjective, just like pain or anxiety. Two people could go through the same situation and have completely different perceptions, reactions, and outcomes. Here is what it stands for (my book *PIVOT; With My 6-Step Crisis Plan* explains it in depth):

C - Confront the crisis and develop coping skills
R - Reframe thoughts, remove negativity, and reflect
I - Identify and assess your situation
S - Set healthy internal and external boundaries
I - Implement the plan and evaluate effectiveness
S - Silver linings, smiling, and serotonin

The significance of this plan is that even in the darkest moments, there is something to hold onto—strength gained, lessons learned, faith deepened. Tying all six steps together and seeking silver linings helps to shift your focus from despair to hope. And yes, smiling truly boosts serotonin, helping to regulate our mood and increase resilience. The simple act of finding joy, even when it feels impossible, changes your brain chemistry. This is easier said than done, but when you think of this more as a daily habit and challenge yourself to find a silver lining even in a "bad" situation, you will truly begin to notice a change in your mindset. I challenge you to write down or think of at least one silver lining every single day, no matter how "bad" it is. And then smile as you think of it.

Having a personal *C.R.I.S.I.S. Plan* in place *before* a crisis occurs isn't just about surviving—it's about learning how to recognize what you are able to control, setting boundaries that are realistic and appropriate for *your* life, and actively transforming pain into strength. You may find some guidance with this by praying the Serenity Prayer daily:

God, grant me the serenity to accept the things I cannot change, courage to change the things I can, and wisdom to know the difference.

Having a plan in place and identifying these principles allows us to be proactive and ready when things go wrong. Because it's not a matter of *if* but *when* we will be staring a crisis in the face. Let's not wait until we have a mental breakdown; we should prepare ourselves by practicing simple, healthy daily habits that can be initiated immediately. Taking a short walk, stretching to get your body moving, or setting aside even ten minutes each day for journaling, prayer, or reflection can be life-changing. Start to build your own *C.R.I.S.I.S. plan* by pinpointing where you feel stuck. Identify your goals, then break them into small, actionable steps that align with your faith or life. Try to focus on one small thing each day, at least initially.

The anger and hurt from a divorce— whether it's yours, your parents' or even your grandparents'—can feel overwhelming and unrelenting. Just like with all grief, everyone moves through the stages differently. There's no timeline for healing, and it's different for everyone. One of the most important things you can do is give yourself grace. Let yourself feel the emotions as they come, without judgment, and remember: *It's okay to not be okay. And you don't have to go through this alone.*

ABOUT THE AUTHOR

Christen Bryce, MS, RN, PMH-BC, is a Catholic single mother of two daughters, a board-certified psychiatric nurse, author, mentor, and Executive Contributor for Brainz Magazine. She currently works full-time in an outpatient mental health clinic and was recently elected Secretary of her local chapter of the National Alliance on Mental Illness (NAMI), deepening her commitment to advocacy and community support.

As founder of The Crisis Nurse, Christen specializes in faith-based generational healing and mental wellness, empowering adult children of late-life (grey) divorce to break cycles before they repeat. Her signature 6-Step CRISIS Plan—featured in her debut book *PIVOT: With My 6-Step Crisis Plan*—offers a proactive framework for emotional and psychological well-being, rooted in Rational Emotive Behavioral Coaching and preventative care.

Christen works directly with clients using this framework to address mental health and relationship challenges, blending clinical insight with spiritual resilience. Through education, mentorship, and advocacy, she equips others to build emotional strength, embrace self-care, and lead more fulfilling lives.

She is an author of *MENtal* Health (Red Thread Publishing, October 2025), a collaborative book exploring men's mental health. Her solo book and companion journal are available now.

Connect:
www.thecrisisnurse.com
www.linktr.ee/christenbryce_rn

Epilogue
WHOLE AFTER ALL

There is no single story of divorce, only a thousand shades of heartbreak and rebirth. Within these pages, we've witnessed women walk through fire: the chaos of addiction, the devastation of betrayal, the exhaustion of abuse, and the quiet unraveling of partnerships that simply couldn't hold any longer. We've heard from daughters still healing the wounds of their parents' separations, from women navigating "gray divorce" after decades of marriage, and from those who managed to part with grace, gratitude, and love still intact.

What unites these stories isn't the split itself; it's what came after. It's the moment each woman decided that survival was not enough, that she and her family deserved to live, not just endure. It's the power in saying *no more* and the courage in saying *I still believe in love, in myself, in tomorrow.*

These women are not broken. They are architects of new beginnings. They've shown that ending a marriage can be an act of protection, a radical form of self-respect, and sometimes, the greatest gift a mother can give her children, a model of courage, integrity, and truth.

Family doesn't end with divorce; it reshapes itself. Love doesn't disappear; it evolves. Wholeness isn't found in maintaining appearances but in living authentically, even when it means stepping into the unknown.

May these stories remind you that choosing yourself and your peace is not destruction; it's devotion. May you carry forward the truth that we are not broken. We are becoming. And so are you.

Thank You

Enjoyed *The Split*?

Your feedback means the world to us!

If the book resonated with you, inspired you, or offered some-thing meaningful, we'd truly appreciate it if you left a **review on Amazon** tinyurl.com/2zemn77d or **GoodReads**. Your feedback helps others discover the book—and it directly supports the author's work.

Acknowledgments

This book is the brainchild of **Brandee Melcher**, whose vision and determination brought *The Split* to life. We are each deeply grateful for the opportunity to be co-authors in this bold and necessary project.

Our heartfelt thanks go to **Dr. Katherine Humphreys**, whose mentorship, insight, and steadfast guidance helped shape this collection into the powerful book it has become.

To every brave woman who contributed her story; thank you. Your honesty, vulnerability, and courage make this work what it is: a testament to resilience, transformation, and truth.

With appreciation to **Mimi Rich** for her dedication and support, and to **Stacy Dyson**, our editor, for her thoughtful eye and care in bringing each story to its fullest expression.

Together, we have created something that speaks to the strength that lives in all of us.

About the Publisher

Red Thread Publishing is an award-winning indie press dedicated to amplifying powerful, authentic nonfiction voices. In our first five years, we've published more than 72 books, supported over 350 authors from 30 countries, and celebrated 41 book awards, proof of the impact and quality behind every title we produce.

Our passionate team is committed to guiding authors through every step of the writing and publishing journey so their stories not only get published but make a lasting impact.

If you want to **write & publish with us** please reach out.

Visit **www.redthreadbooks.com**
Email us **info@redthreadbooks.com**

instagram.com/redthreadbooks
facebook.com/redthreadpublishing
goodreads.com/sierra-melcher
amazon.com/author/sierramelcher

Other Books

COLLABORATIVE RED THREAD ANTHOLOGIES

Taboo: Stories That Can't Be Told

Unflinching yet intimate, *Taboo: Stories That Can't Be Told* gathers voices that give language to pain, prejudice, and resilience—inviting us to dismantle the walls of silence we build around the unspeakable.

Winner of the American Legacy Book Awards, Firebird Awards and Literary Titan Book Awards

~

Planting the Seed: Lessons to Cultivate a Brighter Future

Planting the Seed weaves together intimate, courageous stories from women who have faced deep adversity—infidelity, illness, injustice, and more—and emerged resilient, wise, and ready to grow. Each narrative is a seed of hope, offering lessons in strength, transformation, and the promise of a brighter tomorrow.

Winner of the Nautilus Book Award: Silver Prize in Rising to the Moment 2024

Sactuary: Cultivating Safe Space in Sisterhood; Rediscovering the Power that Unites Us

Sanctuary presents vivid narratives of vulnerability and restoration, showing how sisterhood can become a sacred space where women reclaim voice, belonging, and collective strength.

Winner of Finalist in the American Writing Awards 2024

SPARK: Women in the Business of Changing the World

is a powerful collection of voices from women across the globe, sharing how they're leading with purpose, ambition, and heart.

Winner of the Bronze Global Book Awards, Women in Business 2025

WWW.REDTHREADBOOKS.COM

Notes From Motherland: The Wild Adventure of Raising Humans

In *Notes From Motherland*, each story serves as a window into the unpredictable journey of raising children—navigating hope, heartbreak, growth, and resilience in the day-to-day.

Winner of the Literary Titan Book Awards 2024

∼

FEISTY: Dangerously Amazing Women Using Their Voices & Making An Impact

Bold, raw, and unapologetic, *FEISTY* invites readers into the fire of female power, spotlighting voices that demand to be heard—and showing how courage becomes impact.

Winner of the Literary Titan Book Awards 2025

∼

MENtal Health: Take it "Like a Man"

In *MENtal Health: Take It "Like a Man"*, each narrative becomes a courageous testimony, unfiltered and raw, challenging traditional ideas of masculinity by showing how vulnerability and recovery are essential steps toward wholeness.

Winner of the Literary Titan Book Awards 2025

The Anatomy of a Book

A definitive guide for aspiring authors, featuring insights from 20 industry veterans on writing, publishing, and book marketing. Whether you're new to writing or aiming to elevate your publishing efforts, this anthology offers practical, behind-the-scenes wisdom to help bring your book into the world.

Winner of International Impact Book Awards 2025

By the Light of the Moon

A luminous anthology of personal stories from women who lean into the power and mystery of the feminine.

Winner of the Firebird Awards 2024

Typo: The Art of Imperfect Creation

A compassionate guide for writers, giving you permission to embrace messiness as you begin your story. It offers exercises, insights, and encouragement to help you transform what feels broken or chaotic into something meaningful, daring, and uniquely your own.

Winner of the Nautilus Book Award: Gold Prize in Creativity and Innovation 2024

www.ingramcontent.com/pod-product-compliance
Lightning Source LLC
Chambersburg PA
CBHW020547030426
42337CB00013B/992